Technical Analysis Applications

"The precious timing of an investment could be crucial, especially in the upcoming post-pandemic period affected by higher volatility in financial markets. Among others, due to the possibility of increasing inflation, investing will be a frequent topic. On the issues of technical analysis, I appreciate its comparison with the fundamental analysis, which is often overlooked in the literature. This book brings interesting knowledge to those who are willing to use highly developed applications by financial institutions. However, it is well written even if you are just a beginner in the financial market."

—Ing. Tomas Heryan, Ph.D., *Department of Finance and Accounting, Silesian University, School of Business Administration, Karvina, Czech Republic*

"The topic that is planned to be discussed in this scientific text is very actual and crucial to solve nowadays. In this handbook it will be analyzed the technical analysis implications from the following perspectives: fundamental notions of technical analyses, fundamental analysis versus technical analysis, charts used in technical analysis, important graphical elements used in technical analysis, indicators and oscillators used in technical analysis, correlation between securities and markets, stock exchange predictions, sequential stock market strategies used in technical analysis.

The scope of this textbook is dealing with economy, informatics, from my point of view mostly with economical engineering and quantitative mathematics. I find it as a very useful tool to move forward in this scope of science, that *I strongly recommend to publish this book as a scientific text in year 2023.*"

—Assoc. Prof. Miroslav Škoda, *Vice rector for international relations, DTI University, Slovakia*

"This handbook contains analysis of the technical implications from the following perspectives: fundamental notions of technical analysis; fundamental analysis versus technical analysis; charts used in technical analyses; important graphical elements used in technical analysis; indicators and oscillators used in technical analysis.

In this book, correlations between securities and markets have been critically analyzed. It is also expedient to mention that stock exchange predictions and implications are well explained with various techniques.

Finally, sequential stock market strategies used in technical analysis is also discussed."

—Cordelia Onyinyechi Omodero Ph.D., ACA, *Lecturer at the Department of Accounting, College of Management and Social Sciences, Covenant University Ota, Ogun State, Nigeria*

"As a seasoned industry leader with a distinguished career as CEO of a brokerage firm and serving on the board of the stock exchange, I have a deep appreciation for the crucial role of technical analysis in the financial world. I am proud to introduce this book, which provides a comprehensive and insightful examination of the topic of technical analysis applications. The author's expertise is evident in the clear and practical examples presented, making this an essential resource for traders at any stage of their careers. Whether you are seeking to expand your knowledge of technical analysis or are just starting your journey in finance, this book will provide you with a solid foundation of both theoretical principles and practical applications. I strongly endorse this book and highly recommend it to anyone seeking to enhance their proficiency in the field of technical analysis."

—Molnar Octavian, *CEO of IFB Finwest SA brokerage company, Member—Board of Governors of the Bucharest Stock Exchange, Romania*

Florin Cornel Dumiter · Florin Marius Turcaș

Technical Analysis Applications

A Practical and Empirical Stock Market Guide

palgrave
macmillan

Florin Cornel Dumiter
Department of Economic
and Technical Sciences
Vasile Goldis Western
University of Arad
Arad, Romania

Florin Marius Turcaş
ANEVAR
Romanian Valuators Association
Arad, Romania

ISBN 978-3-031-27415-2 ISBN 978-3-031-27416-9 (eBook)
https://doi.org/10.1007/978-3-031-27416-9

This Palgrave Macmillan imprint is published by the registered company Springer Nature Switzerland AG
The registered company address is: Gewerbestrasse 11, 6330 Cham, Switzerland

For Alina, Letiţia and Marina.
Florin Cornel Dumiter

For Daniela and Marius.
Florin Marius Turcaş

Foreword

"There are hundreds of books in the border discipline of financial market. However, most of them are too theoretical to be read outside the community of experts and scholars. As a result, people outside academia, miss out the benefits that come from having good grasp of issues related to financial market. To help the non-experts contend with this shortcoming in the existing literature, Florin Cornel Dumiter and Florin Marius Turcas delivers an excellent practical guide for financial market, written in easy and understandable style. TECHNICAL ANALYSIS APLLICATIONS. A PRACTICAL AND EMPIRICAL STOCK MARKET GUIDE will certainly be a definitive work for those seeking to master the basics of stock market. Indeed, it is a welcome contribution to the available literature and will deepen reader's understanding of some hotly debated issues related to financial market.

This book is best for technical analysis since it contains an exhaustive amount of information covering the core concepts. The book is neatly well structured and takes technical analysis implications from various perspectives including fundamental notions of technical analysis; fundamental analysis versus technical analyses, charter used in technical analyses; important technical analysis; indicators and oscillators used in technical analysis; correlations between securities and markets; stock exchange rate predictions; sequential stock market strategies used in technical analysis. Despite the wide breadth of knowledge, the book is very approachable and easy to understand for novice traders.

In conclusion, it provides a great introduction to technical analysis. It reads like a textbook explaining everything there is to learn about technical analysis. It provides all the nuts and bolts on which we can build upon. It gives a new angle to view the market, comprises of everything you need to know in stock markets. For the new reader who has no idea about trading and how it works, this book is very thorough from start to end to giving the information one needs if they are new to markets. From how to read charts to understanding indicator and the crucial role technical analysis plays in investing, readers gain a through and accessible overview of the field of technical analysis, with special emphasis on future markets. This book is essential reading for anyone interested in tracking and analyzing market behavior".

Imtiyaz Ahmad Shah
Faculty at Cluster University
of Srinagar
Srinagar, India

Preface

Technical analysis is used, without exception, by analysts, brokers, traders, consultants, and investors. Considered far too primitive and empirical, technical analysis itself has been neglected, *per se*, by academia and theorists. With the development of computational techniques, technical analysis has become increasingly easy to fit into mathematical models.

The aim of this book is not to idolize technical analysis, but to present it with its pluses and minuses; at the same time, we intended to mention other approaches, so that whoever is inquisitive can access them.

The academic community is slowly but surely beginning to recognize the importance of technical analysis in explaining the mechanisms of price formation of listed securities.

Frequently, technical analysis is seen in contradiction with fundamental analysis—the economic-financial analysis of the issuer. We find it very difficult to reconcile balance sheet, degree of indebtedness, or the operational turnover considerations with the stock market performance of securities. That is why some rhetorical questions need to be asked: How many of the dozens of indicators used in financial analysis are needed to try to assess stock market performance? Certainly not all; but which ones are not relevant? What company news influences the market? If you follow the headlines in the press, half of them are "due to the fact that .... ", half "despite the fact that ..., however ... ".

Analyzing the literature, we could see a plethora of books dealing with technical analysis. Some of these successful books will be included and mentioned throughout this handbook and in the references section. However, we ask ourselves: Do we need another book? What does it bring new? What is expected of a new book in the field?

All technical analysis books studied focus *exclusively* on technical analysis. This handbook aims to integrate technical analysis into the much broader field of stock market theses: stock market theories, valuation approaches, portfolio theories, and company analysis. In this way, in addition to deepening technical analysis, the reader will be challenged to learn about alternative, sometimes even contrary, theories and explore related areas in the context of increasing investment efficiency. Unlike other works, this approach does not regard technical analysis as the ultimate and absolute truth and recognizes that by studying all aspects of an interdisciplinary problem, the chances of success substantially increase.

In this handbook, we will try to integrate technical analysis into the wider field of stock market investments, to link it to portfolio theory, valuation theories, and other modern approaches: behavior, game theory, and complex statistical theories (machine learning, genetic algorithms). In addition, we will guide the interested reader to further documentation. This handbook will provide the background for exploring cutting-edge areas (econophysics, fractal theories, etc.) in conjunction with technical analysis.

It is our hope that the summary covers the basic questions that any participant should ask on the stock market:

- What is my investment profile? What type of investments are suitable for me?
- How is the market now? Where is it heading?
- What stocks are underpriced and overpriced? Why, how to price them?
- What stocks are attractive? For what term? What are the optimal entry/exit points?
- How do I build a portfolio? When do I adjust it? How do I control it?
- How do I draw conclusions from successes/shortcomings? What feedback do I get?

The approach covered in this handbook will rely on technical analysis to answer these questions. We will not limit ourselves to interpreting a chart, as most specialized courses do; and we will present other theories, we will not cling to technical analysis as a universal elixir. We will approach the matter interdisciplinary, as it is beneficial and modern in most natural sciences and society.

We are not aware of a similar approach to the correlation of different theories and/or methods related to stock markets. We will initiate these connections, convinced that the emphasis of practitioners on technical analysis, theorists on statistical analysis, economists on fundamental analysis, and valuators on specific approaches must all ultimately come together in a unified vision to help the retail investor make informed and justified decisions as rationally as possible. And, perhaps we have unduly left out psychologists and/or sociologists; but this is not our area of expertise, and we invite any specialist to a dialogue about the specific elements that need to be taken into account when tackling a subject as complex as stock market behavior.

Chapter 1 presents the introductory aspects and the sine qua non-conditions and prerequisites regarding the assessment of the technical analysis. Chapter 2 deals with the dichotomy of technical analysis versus fundamental analysis by revealing some interesting and actual practical aspects. Chapter 3 tackles the most important correlation between different types of securities and several markets. Chapter 4 brings forward the most important steps in the construction of several types of charts frequently used in technical analysis. Chapter 5 encompasses the main important graphic elements used in technical analysis in a logical pattern agenda. Chapter 6 analyzes several indicators and oscillators used in theory and practice. Chapter 7 highlights the important role of forecasts manifested in the stock market. Finally, Chapter 8 evaluates and assesses the investment strategies arranged in a sequential orientation used in technical analysis.

Arad, Romania
December 2022

Florin Cornel Dumiter
Florin Marius Turcaş

Acknowledgements

Technical analysis allows innovation but is not substantial. We did not set out to revolutionize the field, but we are not very traditionalists either.

Compared to other specialists, we do not consider technical analysis as absolute truth. It has many advantages and good parts, but it also has flaws, shortcomings, inexplicable situations. We will not hesitate to point out the weaknesses and the parts not covered by the study of charts. We will present other theories, albeit briefly. We think it is only normal that readers should be informed and to be able to go down on alternative paths to technical analysis.

We will not take an exhaustive and complete approach to technical analysis. We will direct the interested reader to a rich bibliography in every direction, but we will not detail the parts that we do not trust for the sake of completeness of the book. This is the case of the Elliot wave, which, in our opinion, say nothing and which we will present only briefly, enumerative. However, we will point to relevant sources of documentation in the field.

We would like to thank our colleague from the Faculty of Socio Humanity Sciences of the Vasile Goldiş Western University of Arad, Laura Rebeca Stiegelbauer for the continuous partnership, implication and support regarding the English translation and language supervision of our handbook.

Interesting recommendations and insightful comments and suggestions were provided by our colleagues from the Department of Economic and Technical Department, Faculty of Economics, Computer Sciences and Engineering of the Vasile Goldiş Western University of Arad.

Special merit is recognized for Diana Jalbă—Product Manager of Information for the implication, suggestions, support and continue partnership regarding the book proposal, evaluation, and acceptance process.

Special thanks are due to the entire Springer Nature and Palgrave Macmillan teams for the dedication and implication regarding our book project, especially Ananda Kumar Mariappan, Tula Weis, Faith Su and Wyndham Hacket Pain.

Florin Cornel Dumiter
Florin Marius Turcaş

Translator's Note

This is also a good lesson in patience. A new investor or trader usually lacks patience and has the tendency to want to jump in, fearful of missing out on an advantage. Don't make that mistake. Wait for the confirmation. Buy at the bottom, not at the top. And, always use a Stop Loss to protect your capital. "Nothing gives one person so much advantage over another as to remain cool and unruffled under all circumstances."—Thomas Jefferson

—Fred McAllen, Charting and Technical Analysis

I was very happy when my colleagues Florin Cornel and Florin Marius invited me to join this special handbook project. In the aftermath of the first book, Florin Cornel et al. (2021) published on pension systems, I knew that this next project will be more interesting and challenging.

The financial market is the most exciting area of enrichment in the cutting-edge research agenda addressed by contemporary economics. Within this vast field, the stock market is a very interesting and challenging domain. In this respect, the terminology used in this handbook was handled in three specific ways. First, the stock market, *lato sensu*, and technical analysis, *stricto sensu*, must comprise a specific and technical vocabulary well recognized and used in the finance domain. Second, the multidisciplinary approach strategy carried out by the authors raised another set of terminology due to the connections with several fields such as mathematics, econophysics, and natural sciences. Finally, the practical case studies, graphical representations and analyses, the econometric modeling techniques applied to the stock market, and technical analysis were very complex and require a high degree of coherence and robustness in order to present the empirical research in a comprehensive manner.

I am trustful that the translation supervision of this handbook will be useful for academics and practitioners in deciphering the multifaceted trajectories of stock markets, especially in cases of turbulent and volatile economic environment that we face nowadays. Accordingly, I believe that the linguistic fine-tuning adjustments that were made to the manuscript in the first draft will lead to a better understanding of the inter-multi and transdisciplinary approaches *vis – á – vis* of technical analysis adopted by the authors.

Ultimately, this handbook is dedicated to a wide range of specialists, starting with students, master level and Ph.D. candidates, academics in the process of increasing their academic quality skills and techniques, different types of investors operating on the stock market but also for international financial institutions staff in the preparation and specialization training methods. Finally, I think that this handbook is also recommended for the non-specialist people which are interested in deciphering the stock markets' mystical and complex characteristics.

December 2022

Laura Rebeca Stiegelbauer
Vasile Goldiş Western University
of Arad
Arad, Romania

Contents

About the Authors

Florin Cornel Dumiter is Full Professor of Finance at the Department of Economics and Technical Sciences, Faculty of Economics, Engineering and Informatics at "Vasile Goldiş" Western University of Arad. He holds an economist and legal adviser diploma and received a Ph.D. in Finance and a Ph.D. in Tax Law at the West University of Timişoara and a Postdoctoral Degree in Economics at the Romanian Academy. His research interests include international finance, international capital markets, finance and banking, tax, banking, and capital market law. He published 4 books at international publishers and 10 books at national publishers, over 80 articles indexed in Clarivate Analytics, Scopus, and other important international databases. The courses and seminars he teaches are Public Finance, Monetary Economics, Assurance Management at bachelor level, and Financial Markets and Financial Management at master level. In recent years, he has also taught courses and seminars regarding tax law and business law. He is also a practitioner activated as a chartered accountant and tax consultant and adviser, and also he has judicial and accounting, and fiscal expertise. He is Editor-in-Chief of Studia Universitatis "Vasile Goldiş" Arad—Economics Series which is indexed in 35 international databases including Claryvate Analytics and Scopus and Managing Editor of Journal of Legal Studies indexed in 30 international databases, both journals are published under DeGruyter (Sciendo) Publishing House.

Florin Marius Turcaş holds both an economist and engineer degree. He is also an appraiser at ANEVAR with specializations in real estate, enterprises, financial assets, a judicial expert in the field of immovable properties, a financial analyst for BSE at IFB Finwest SA (top 10 brokers on BSE), an investment, and funding and corporate operations consultant (M&A, spin-offs, public offerings). Starting from 2005 he is a recognized technical analyses practician. Research activities include articles and publications in recognized journals indexed in multiple international databases including Claryvate Analytics and Scopus.

List of Figures

List of Tables

CHAPTER 1

Fundamental Notions of Technical Analysis

Abstract In its simplest form, technical analysis consists of plotting the stock market performance of securities prices and the use of patterns, indicators, and oscillators in order to predict future evolution. In more complex forms, any process that considers price movements to be decisive (at the expense of the issuer's financial data) can be considered as belonging to technical analysis. Technical analysis, modern portfolio theory, and valuation by market comparison—all these are based on the informational efficiency of the market (Fama): the price reflects all the necessary information about a company. What can be observed is easy to guess: the price varies according to the struggle between buyers (who want as low a price as possible) and sellers (who want a price as high as possible) even when nothing happens in the company in order to justify the change. Some theories consider the trajectory of stocks to be arbitrary (random walk). Obviously, this would mean that their evolution cannot be predicted, thwarting any predictive effort. While it is true that no accurate predictions can be made, the evolution may not be random: the order of magnitude depends on the financial characteristics of the issuer, the drunkenness walk shows that statistics can be applied even if the movement is disordered (Brownian), when the market trend is strong it is not hard to anticipate that it will attract many issuers, etc. The autoregressive theories AR, ARMA, ARIMA, etc., and ARCH, GARCH, etc., attempt to demonstrate the unpredictability of the stock market evolution—we will review them. Technical analysis provides a very eloquent

F. C. Dumiter and F. M. Turcaş, *Technical Analysis Applications*,
https://doi.org/10.1007/978-3-031-27416-9_1

graphical insight on the evolution of a security. On any stock exchange in the world, if you opened the electronic platform of a company it can be seen the chart of recent evolution. Regardless of the context, an analysis is not complete if it does not present these charts, even if only for information. There is no broker or trader who does not look at the chart before initiating a trade; there is no consultant or analyst who does not present these graphs to a client. Technical analysis alone cannot explain or predict an issuer's evolution. Try to predict the movement of a security on chartgame.com, even in competition with a professional technical analyst and you will see that the chances of winning are equal. On its own, without market or company information, technical analysis is not a magic mirror that predicts the future based on past performance.

Keywords Graphical representation · Informational efficiency · Random walk · Autoregressive theories · Chart evolution

1.1 Defining Technical Analysis

Technical analysis is one of the most widely used and complex technique that investor employ nowadays to achieve profit and success in the investment process. In modern finance, technical analysis is seen as one of the *mystical* techniques as it represents a situation in which both the art and science parts are present.

Graphical representation is the oldest way of analyzing the evolution of some stock quotes. It is simple, easy to understand and use and extremely expressive ("a picture is worth 1000 words"). Try to explain in words the evolution of the stock below (Fig. 1.1):

Or explain the events and their consequences without using the chart: "on 21.02.2020 opened at 2.0537, peaked at 2.0579 and closed on a minimum of 1.9008, thus breaking a high upward trend that clearly results from the Table 1.1 (bvb.ro): "…

… alternative being the visual—the drawing of the blue line on the chart.

Although much more intuitive and easier to understand than any other mathematical approach, technical analysis has been considered an *esoteric* technique by academia, articles, and academic books have dismissed it as unscientific. This created a fracture between the theory learned from the

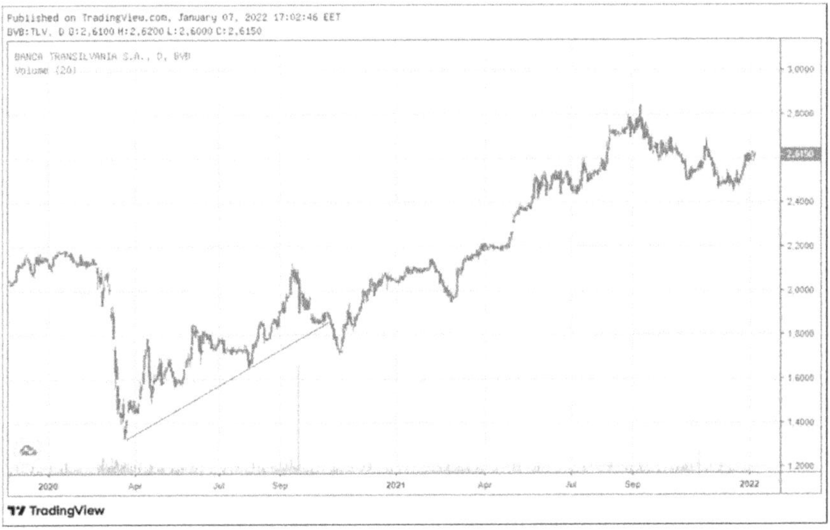

Fig. 1.1 TLV stock at BSE chart evolution (*Source* https://bvb.ro/FinancialInstruments/Details/FinancialInstrumentsDetails.aspx?s=TLV)

everyday academic approach of business schools where brokers, traders, and investors especially followed market trends and charts and reacted to technical analysis signals. Recent developments in computational techniques that translate graphical models into mathematical models, as well as the integration of statistical models, have led to a rethinking of the role of technical analysis and a worldwide recognition of its importance in stock price movements.

1.2 Wave Movement (Trends) Versus Random Walk: Dow Theory

Dow theory states that prices move in waves, in trends. In practice, we often use this kind of expression: the economy is doing well, a period of economic boom, crisis, and economic collapse.

The best analogy is with the weather. We know the summer will be hot and we prepare for it. It is not out of the question to have storms, cool days, or even unexpected weather events. But by and large, when summer comes, we prepare for the heat.

Table 1.1 TLV trading data

Data	*Volume*	*Open*	*Min*	*Max*	*Average*	*Close*	*Var. (%)*
18.09.2020	116,772,958	2.5250	2.4600	2.5400	2.4650	2.4600	−1.60
17.09.2020	6,517,401	2.4850	2.4650	2.5250	2.4850	2.5000	0.20
16.09.2020	6,746,008	2.5400	2.4600	2.5400	2.5000	2.4950	−1.58
15.09.2020	7,532,647	2.5350	2.5050	2.5500	2.5250	2.5350	0.00
14.09.2020	10,372,921	2.5000	2.4900	2.5700	2.5450	2.5350	1.40
11.09.2020	14,932,573	2.4000	2.4000	2.5000	2.4700	2.5000	4.60
10.09.2020	5,137,786	2.3900	2.3900	2.4100	2.3950	2.3900	0.21
09.09.2020	6,214,866	2.3900	2.3800	2.3950	2.3850	2.3850	−0.42
08.09.2020	10,360,650	2.3650	2.3650	2.4050	2.3950	2.3950	1.48
07.09.2020	6,505,364	2.3100	2.3100	2.3600	2.3400	2.3600	2.61
04.09.2020	6,791,199	2.3250	2.3000	2.3600	2.3400	2.3000	−2.34
03.09.2020	5,926,039	2.3150	2.3000	2.3650	2.3350	2.3550	1.95
02.09.2020	5,958,368	2.3100	2.2950	2.3150	2.3050	2.3100	0.00
01.09.2020	12,566,432	2.2900	2.2750	2.3100	2.3000	2.3100	1.09
31.08.2020	6,578,097	2.2250	2.2150	2.2850	2.2650	2.2850	2.70
28.08.2020	5,340,212	2.2500	2.2100	2.2600	2.2250	2.2250	−1.33
27.08.2020	4,270,042	2.2650	2.2400	2.2700	2.2550	2.2550	−0.44
26.08.2020	4,804,375	2.2450	2.2450	2.2700	2.2550	2.2650	0.67
25.08.2020	8,725,216	2.2400	2.2400	2.2700	2.2550	2.2500	0.90
24.08.2020	7,176,812	2.1900	2.1850	2.2450	2.2300	2.2300	1.83
21.08.2020	1,847,631	2.1600	2.1500	2.1900	2.1600	2.1900	1.39
20.08.2020	2,340,385	2.1600	2.1450	2.1600	2.1550	2.1600	0.47
19.08.2020	2,702,959	2.1500	2.1400	2.1600	2.1500	2.1500	0.00
18.08.2020	2,681,741	2.1600	2.1400	2.1600	2.1550	2.1500	−0.46
17.08.2020	5,904,316	2.2150	2.1300	2.2150	2.1550	2.1600	−2.92
14.08.2020	6,982,448	2.2450	2.2150	2.2450	2.2250	2.2250	−0.67
13.08.2020	5,997,069	2.2450	2.2300	2.2550	2.2500	2.2400	−0.44
12.08.2020	4,564,942	2.2150	2.2150	2.2500	2.2350	2.2500	1.58
11.08.2020	7,850,069	2.1600	2.1600	2.2350	2.2100	2.2150	2.07
10.08.2020	894,219	2.1450	2.1450	2.1700	2.1600	2.1700	0.93
07.08.2020	3,295,947	2.1100	2.1100	2.1500	2.1250	2.1500	0.94
06.08.2020	1,626,020	2.1300	2.0950	2.1350	2.1200	2.1300	0.00
05.08.2020	12,475,485	2.0800	2.0750	2.1300	2.1050	2.1300	2.40
04.08.2020	1,114,885	2.0200	2.0200	2.0900	2.0700	2.0800	2.97
03.08.2020	1,521,840	2.0400	2.0050	2.0400	2.0200	2.0200	1.00
31.07.2020	2,355,979	2.0350	2.0000	2.0750	2.0250	2.0000	−1.72

Source https://bvb.ro/FinancialInstruments/Details/FinancialInstrumentsDetails.aspx?s=TLV

The economy, and with it the stock markets, also go through similar movements: periods of boom (bull market) and periods of bust (bear market). This is easy to see if you look at the Dow Jones chart over the last half century. The Dow Jones is an index of the best American companies (blue chips); its value is obtained by adding up prices of the companies forming it (Fig. 1.2).

It is clear that there are times when the market has momentum (trending), there are periods of stagnation (flat trading) and there are times of decline, of crisis. This in itself would not be a demonstration that stocks move in waves: it may just be random periodicities. The demonstration is given by the fact that these trends behave like sea waves: they take everything with them, nothing can stop them. For example, in 2021, we were on a strong upward trend, and in the Fig. 1.3 we can see that most companies are also on an upward trend. On contrary, 2022 was a bad stock exchange year, with big companies market value dropping.

However, this is an undeniable advantage of technical analysis: it succeeds, with remarkable accuracy, to pinpoint trends, give signals of overheating and trend reversals, and predict certain market movements. This is also why it is used in automated trading: signals are detected by computers and trades are made on their basis, without human intervention.

Fig. 1.2 American market trends (*Source* https://www.investing.com/indices/us-30-chart)

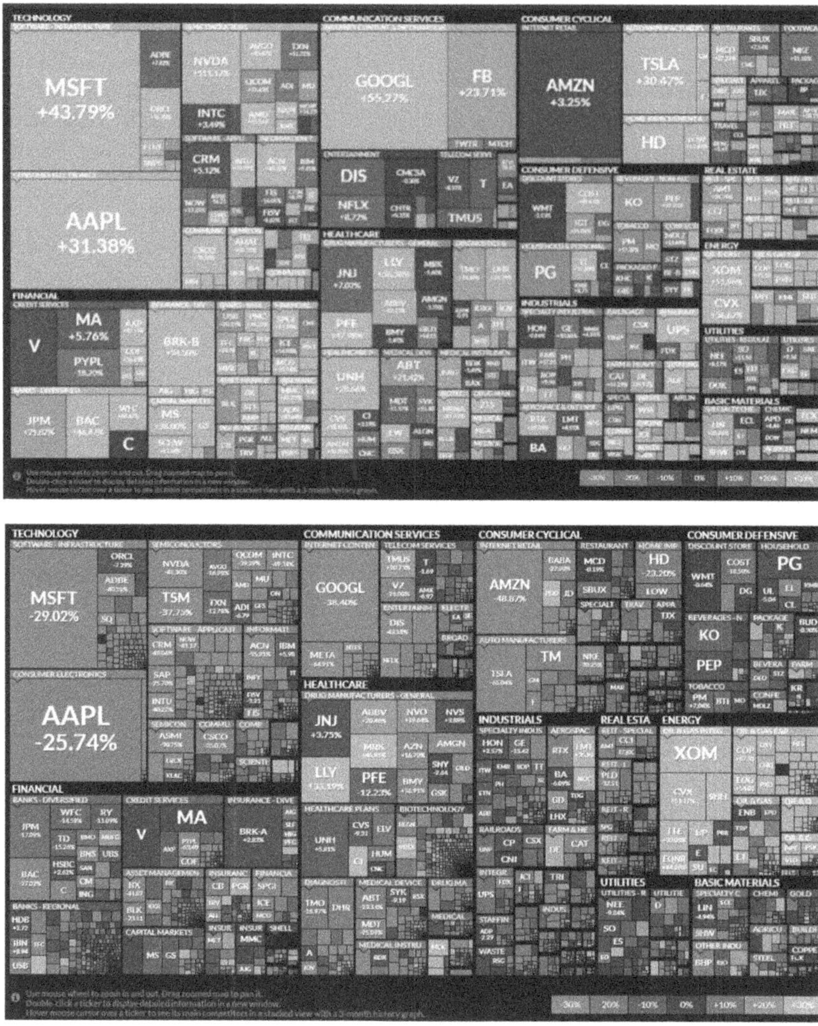

Fig. 1.3 American stock market developments map in 2021 vs 2022 (*Source* https://finviz.com/map.ashx?t=sec&st=w52)

The contrary theory states that price changes are random, and therefore, cannot be predicted. Obviously, in this disappointing case, any analysis of the markets would be useless, as it does not lead to a reliable forecast of future developments.

It should be noted that there is also some truth in the statement that developments cannot be predicted. We cannot know whether a stock will rise, stagnate or fall tomorrow, or by how much. The same chart above, extended to the day level, shows that even in the strongest positive (upward) trend, there are contraction days and even full periods of decline (Fig. 1.4).

Proponents of random walk theory use autoregressive mathematical methods to prove their theory: AR, ARCH, GARCH, ARMA, ARIMA, etc.

The idea is that one cannot predict the price movements of the next day based on previous price movements. In this sense, we can imply that a GARCH model is an autoregressive (autoregressive generalized conditional heteroscedastic) model that determines two polynomials:

- GARCH, compounded from *lagged conditional variance*, of P degree;
- ARCH, compounded from *lagged squared innovations*, of Q degree.

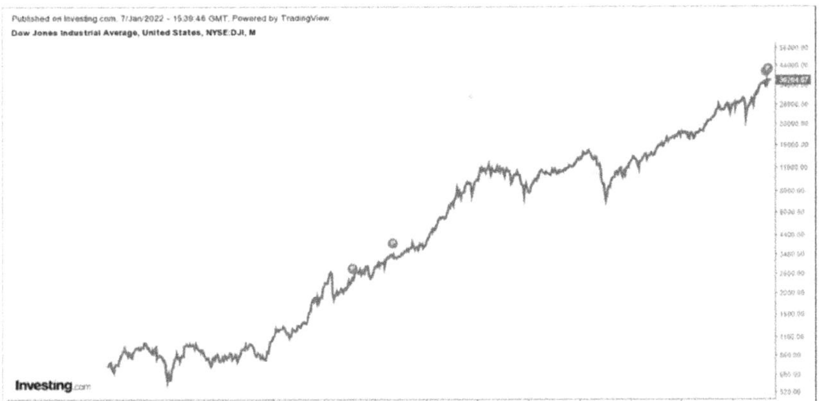

Fig. 1.4 Logarithmic evolution of the American index Dow Jones (*Source* https://www.investing.com/indices/us-30-chart)

The results of the Matlab application function over the history percentage changes (return) of SIF1, starting from 2000 and until 2016 highlight a GARCH (1,1) positive variation (Fig. 1.5):

$$\epsilon_t = 0.8204\sigma_{t-1}^2 + 0.1796\sigma_{t-1}^2 \tag{1.1}$$

with the innovation Gaussian distributed, and:

$$\sigma_t^2 = 1,014.10^{-5} + 0,8204\sigma_{t-1}^2 + 0,1796\epsilon_{t-1}^2 \tag{1.2}$$

The results are graphical confirmed, the innovations have been similar with the returns (Fig. 1.6),

However, the autocorrect function presents inconclusive results for the normally lags (Fig. 1.7):

Analyzing these aspects, we can conclude that similar results have been obtained also in the cases of S&P 500 US (GARCH 0.877 and ARCH 0.1034) and DJIA (GARCH 0.8978 and ARCH 0.0953).

Field	Value	Min	Max
exitFlag	5	5	5
warning	'No Warnings'		
converge	'Function Converged to a Solution'		
constraints	'Boundary Constraints Active: Standard Errors May Be Inaccurate'		
covMatrix	<4x4 double>	-3.3801e-05	4.7918e-05
iterations	21	21	21
functionC...	141	141	141
lambda	<1x1 struct>		

MATLAB Variable Editor: Coeff — Page 1
May 14, 2019 — 12:29:38 PM

Field	Value	Min	Max
Comment	<1x41 char> Mean: ARMAX(0,0,0); Variance: GARCH(1,1)		
Distribution	'Gaussian'		
C	0.0011	0.0011	0.0011
Variance...	'GARCH'		
P	1	1	1
Q	1	1	1
K	1.0140e-05	1.0140e-05	1.0140e-05
GARCH	0.8204	0.8204	0.8204
ARCH	0.1796	0.1796	0.1796

Fig. 1.5 Garchfit results of SIF1 in Matlab (*Source* Own processing)

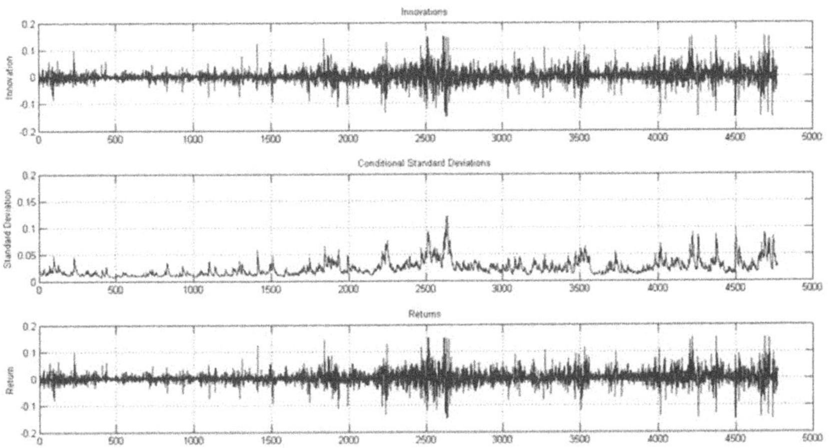

Fig. 1.6 Matlab graph obtained in Matlab for the demonstration of GARCH (1,1) model framing (*Source* Own processing)

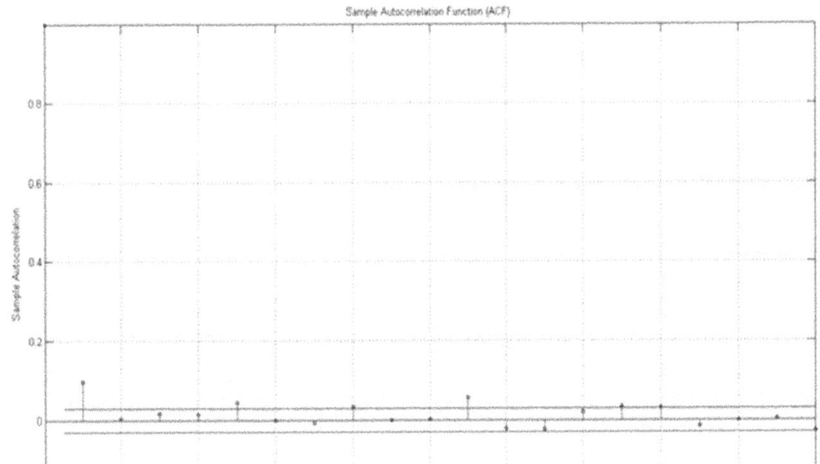

Fig. 1.7 Autocorrelation determined and represented in Matlab (*Source* Own processing)

1.3 Advantages and Disadvantages of Technical Analysis

What is technical analysis based on? On the battle between buyers and sellers, between bid and ask. Some want to buy as cheaply as possible; others want to sell as expensive as possible. From their continuous struggle is born the market price (the current stock price), as a precarious balance, of the moment. That is why technical analysis applies only to liquid companies with good tradability, to which, at any time, there are enough buyers and sellers. And this price fluctuates according to the strength of the parties, the pressure to buy or sell. This also explains the trends: when investors and speculators are enthusiastic, they rush to buy and force the prices up. When panic sets in, many sell regardless of the price, and it collapses (Table 1.2).

The image above shows the trading screen for the issuer TLV, from the Bucharest Stock Exchange (Romania). On the left, bid quotes signify the offer to buy, in descending order of value. On the right, the ask represents the offer to sell, in ascending order of value. For a transaction to take place, either the seller must accept the buyer's price (quotation) or vice versa: the buyer accepts the price demanded by the seller.

This is where the technical analysis comes in: each participant makes their own calculations, analyses, and valuations. Independently of this, you can only trade shares at the market price, but this is given by the multitude of participants; some super qualified, some unsuspecting; some with a lot of money, others with derisory sums; some who speculate for a few minutes, others who want to leave the shares to their grandchildren at retirement. And all intermediate categories; and even arbitrage seekers, who do not even care how the prices will evolve (we will see later why).

And then, a participant basically has two variants: either he uses technical analysis or the fundamental one. We intentionally neglected other esoteric analyses (horoscope genre), although they are treated by the specialized literature.

Alarming is the fact that having a simple google search with the theme: *"astrology + stock"* returns over 14 million results. In this way, the subjective reaction applied to a large scale of participants can determine, overall, a final movement of the stock exchange in the sense of prediction confirmation. This confirmation, through the domino effect, can determine the high confidence of one side of the public regarding the mystical approaches.

Table 1.2 The TLV at BSE trading screen

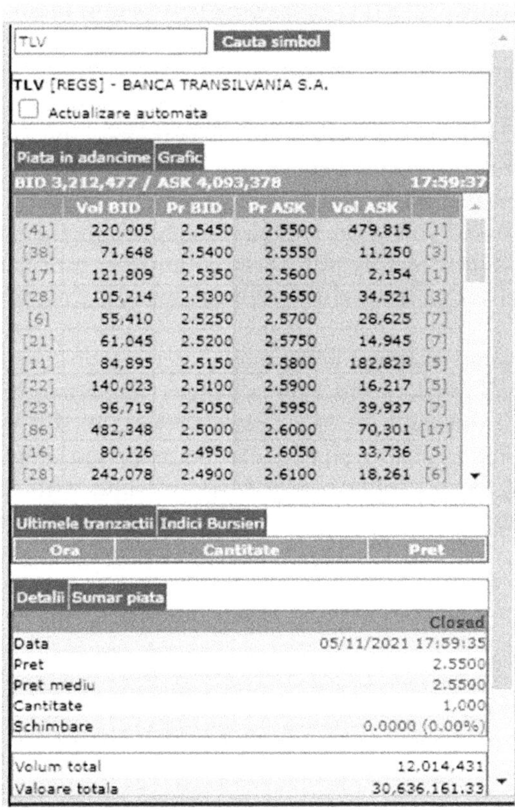

TLV | Cauta simbol

TLV [REGS] - BANCA TRANSILVANIA S.A.

Actualizare automata

Piata in adancime | Grafic

BID 3,212,477 / ASK 4,093,378 17:59:37

	Vol BID	Pr BID	Pr ASK	Vol ASK	
[41]	220,005	2.5450	2.5500	479,815	[1]
[38]	71,648	2.5400	2.5550	11,250	[3]
[17]	121,809	2.5350	2.5600	2,154	[1]
[28]	105,214	2.5300	2.5650	34,521	[3]
[6]	55,410	2.5250	2.5700	28,625	[7]
[21]	61,045	2.5200	2.5750	14,945	[7]
[11]	84,895	2.5150	2.5800	182,823	[5]
[22]	140,023	2.5100	2.5900	16,217	[5]
[23]	96,719	2.5050	2.5950	39,937	[7]
[86]	482,348	2.5000	2.6000	70,301	[17]
[16]	80,126	2.4950	2.6050	33,736	[5]
[28]	242,078	2.4900	2.6100	18,261	[6]

Ultimele tranzactii | Indici Bursieri

Ora	Cantitate	Pret

Detalii | Sumar piata

Closed

Data	05/11/2021 17:59:35
Pret	2.5500
Pret mediu	2.5500
Cantitate	1,000
Schimbare	0.0000 (0.00%)
Volum total	12,014,431
Valoare totala	30,636,161.33

Source https://www.ifbfinwest.ro/index.php#

Technical analysis means to study, mainly graphically, the past evolution of the markets and the title itself and to conclude on the moment of entry/exit. Fundamental analysis means to rely on the financial data (predominantly, but not exclusively: a complete analysis of the company must be carried out) of the issuer, to make a (more or less detailed, professional) valuation of the shares and based on it to make the investment decision.

There are securities in the financial markets where fundamental analysis simply does not work. Cryptocurrencies are the latest example of a form without substance: they are not based on anything in the real economy, yet they have a value (which is given only by trusting them and accepting them by as many economic agents as possible). Nowadays, neither the dollar nor the euro nor other currencies have coverage in gold, oil, or other physical counterparts—they are fiat money. But they are issued by states, which, through their economies, guarantee the sustainability of currencies. Cryptocurrencies behave like issuers without assets, without a balance sheet, and without profit or financial indicators. Well, their trading can be based solely on technical analysis, on the study of trends and reverse moments. Simply put, there is no other rational method! On the bitcoin chart are presented the signals given by the technical analysis (Fig. 1.8).

Another eloquent example is the Forex: betting on foreign exchanges, the EUR/USD quotation undergoes changes depending on the needs in each currency of the millions of economic agents in this world. Broadly speaking, the long-term movements can be predicted, depending on the economic strength and trade in the euro area and with the rest of the world (which largely accepts the US dollar as the universal currency of exchange). But trades in the Forex markets (which are betting markets) are made to the fourth decimal place. Neither the finest connoisseur, nor the most informed banker, nor any trader can predict the evolution of the

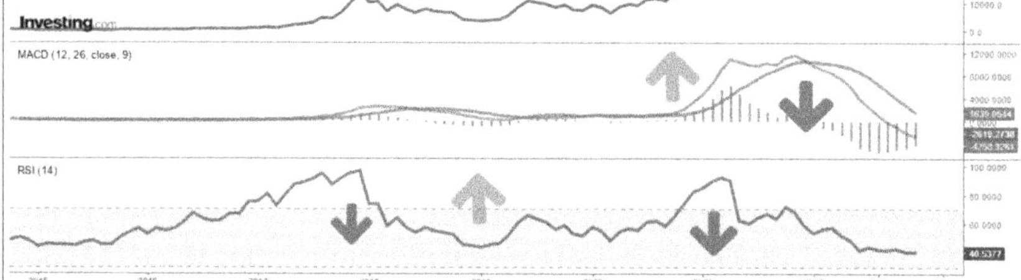

Fig. 1.8 Technical analyses signals on Bitcoin (*Source* https://www.investing.com)

exchange rate, of any currency, to the second and to the decimal place. Therefore, for those who risk trading Forex, technical analysis remains the only solution as rational as possible.

We must insist that technical analysis is based on the free formation of the price, from the continuous struggle between buyers and sellers. For example, on the Romanian market (where Forex transactions are not regulated), the law allows the intervention of the central bank without it being considered market manipulation. Under such conditions, the technical analysis loses its purpose, because the historical graph no longer represents the free evolution of the sum (average) of the opinions of the market participants, but the distorting effect of forced interferences.

It must also be insisted that the market must be strong for technical analysis to make sense, and in a way, each participant tries to manipulate the market, to convince the counter-party to accept its proposed price. An active, reasonably sized market causes these attempts to get lost in the rush of transactions, so that, on the whole, the result validates a main direction of evolution. To apply technical analysis in a market or to a traded anemic security makes no sense because the price evolution can be easily distorted by a few disparate offers (Table 1.3).

Table 1.3 Advantages and disadvantages of technical analysis

Technical analysis advantages	*Technical analysis disadvantages*
It is simple, easy to understand and apply	It is assessed upon the market information efficiency: the price includes all information necessary about the issuer
It is intuitive and does not necessitate prior technical or advanced knowledge	It does not explain the variation due to the financial results or the patrimonial situation of the issuers
It is easy to be implemented in automated trading systems	Contradict the principle according to which the past results do not guarantee future evolutions (this principle must be kept compulsory in any prospect regarding public offer)
Everybody is using this technique, so as to some certain formations are self-confirming: if all analysts agreed that a correction is about to happen, no investor will act against general opinion	It is applicable only to the high degree of liquidity markets and without any manipulations

Source Own processing

The conclusions drawn from the above mentioned table subsumes that technical analysis must not be single applied and it is not either a sacrosanct method of the stock market. Consequently, technical analysis is very useful at the determination of the entry/exit point in/from the market, upon the short-run speculation, and on some markets in which financial analysis is not very comprehensive (i.e., Forex, crypto).

1.4 Technical Analysis in Academia

Technical analysis exists, *mutadis mutandis*, since the enactment of the homogenous products transactions of whose prices deserves the graphical representation.

In this section, we will analyze the most important framework of the technical analyses in the current state of the art enriched in the academic work of different wide scale recognized specialists.

Murphy (1999) represents a classical reference regarding technical analysis applied on the financial market, the last edition of the entire work was the one finished in 1999. The essence of this work is that technical analysis is science, but especially art, the interpretation of the signals representing everything. This study is maintaining its actuality and it is recommended as a starting point for every future specialist.

Brooks (2011) suggests that *computer-generated trading now accounts for as much as 70 percent of the day's volume*. With regard to this problem, it is necessary to build mathematical models using powerful software and also through elaborate theoretical training for those proposing these models. The study developed by Brooks (2011) treats the trading bars of several minutes gathering to the conclusion that successes can be measured only by statistics.

Other studies have focused on the basic techniques of technical analysis. Di Lorenzo (2013) suggests that a new approach is needed regarding the few basic steps for an investor to successfully apply technical analysis in the financial market. This paper discusses the most important steps to be considered by any type of investor in the modern technical analysis process.

In financial market practice, there is a rapid and steady trend of increasingly sophisticated techniques and procedures. Chen (2010) argues that there is a current growing trend toward the development of more accurate and sophisticated technical analysis techniques, especially those of intraday chart analysis.

Thomsett (2012a) reveals several techniques and tactics oriented toward a successful technical analysis process, offering, *ceteris paribus,* a very interesting guide to investors worldwide regarding the steps needed to be taken into account in stock trends. Another interesting study of Thomsett (2012b) is represented by the development of the Bloomberg candlestick charting guide, in which the author generates a comprehensive study by revealing the main parts and advantages of this special technique, especially in regard to technical analysis.

Interest full insights and special techniques regarding strategies used for predicting the financial markets have been analyzed by Greenblatt (2013). In his handbook, the author establishes an interesting guide toward several important techniques such as Elliott wave, Lucas, Fibonacci, Gann, and time profit. The author concludes that these techniques have their own steps which are needed to be respected for a successful investment process.

Tsinaslanidis and Zapranis (2016) developed a new algorithm for pattern recognition regarding the technical analysis process. In their study, the authors conclude that developing rule-based pattern recognizers and different statistical tests can lead to improving the practical and empirical investigation of the entire technical analysis process.

The Ichimoku Clouds technique was analyzed by several specialists. Patel (2010) developed an interesting handbook regarding the importance of Ichimoku Clouds as a fundamental technique in the evaluation and assessment of the technical analysis process. In the aftermath, Linton (2010) developed further improvement in the context of understanding the paths, methods, and implementation process of the Ichimoku Clouds in the context of a successful technical analysis process.

Jimon et al. (2021) highlight the importance of an investment portfolio in which is needed to take into account the risk and uncertainty needed for the investment funds strategy which is needed to be reflected in the financial instruments.

Turcaş et al. (2016) developed a selection of financial assets based on several criteria and concluded that it is necessary to analyze a portfolio as a composite asset. In the aftermath of this study, Turcaş et al. (2017) enable a *quid pro quo* in order to evaluate and assess the optimal and efficient portfolio construction by using several statistical applications on the stock market.

The interesting problem of stock market forecasts and predictions has been addressed by Dumiter and Turcaş (2022). In this study, the authors analyze both theoretically and practically the investor's target and risk using technical analysis methods. The authors conclude that by using several enriched forecasting methods in the investment process, the thorny disadvantages of the current theoretical framework can be eliminated.

Finally, these above mentioned works and studies can subsume technical analysis in both theory and practice and especially in academia. From an empirical field, technical analysis has become a field that can be subsumed as "far too scientific".

1.5 Finis Coronat Opus

Technical analysis exists for centuries: we do not aim to reinvent it in this handbook. However, we intend to present it in a different manner: without any details and irrelevant specifications, but in relationship with other theories such as valuation, portfolio, economic theories, and stock marker ones.

In our opinion, the dictum: KISS (keep it simple, stupid) is applied to technical analysis more than in any other research field. The market depends on a whole range of factors, some of them are strictly mathematical but others are random. The human psychology of feelings and reactions (some of them spontaneous, illogical) is an intrinsic part of it. Market analysis must therefore be enabled on the basis of its precision: it does not have to be too specific, but neither can we pretend that price movements are absolutely random.

Technical analysis cannot be a single tool for understanding and assessing the market. An undated chart reveals nothing, not even to the best technical analysis specialist. The art lies in conferring a *trade-off* between the notion of fundamental analysis of the issuer with the valuation aspects for determining an optimal portfolio correlated with the cognition capacities and investment profile (both financial and psychological) of the investor/speculator.

Summarizing in the theoretical and empirical technical analysis literature we can identify a lot of good and excellent books. There are also blogs, personal, or collective websites related to technical analysis or having a critical perspective. Accordingly, other types of approaches such as Elliott wave, Japanese bands, and Ichimoku clouds can also be identified. All of these are very interesting, but it doesn't mean they will help you if you don't decipher their secrets. These techniques will be discussed with pros and cons in the following sections, but it is not intended to discourage anyone who wishes to apply them if an investor feels they are suitable and appropriate techniques.

In this manual, the shortcomings of technical analysis will be presented, because it is not an absolute and safe profit tool, because if it were and everyone used it, the market would lose its meaning. Everyone who applies technical analysis needs to know the basic principle: *cut your losses out*, let *the profit flow in*. If a losing situation presents itself, it must be acknowledged and exited without hesitation. If we are on the right side of the market, do not exist until the trend reversal is confirmed. The investor shouldn't aim at buying at an absolute low and sell at an all-time high; this situation rarely happens. We recommend buying low and selling high, regardless of the order of trading.

Ultimately, everyone must consider their own risk appetite. In one of our paper presentations at an international conference, someone asked: if we have \$2000, where should we invest it? The answer was the one that every consultant and specialist must give: it depends on your psychological state: what are your expectations? How often do you analyze the market (what is your investment horizon?)? The answer was that in 5 minutes a good specialist can double the initial investment of 2000 USD: you have to be active in the Forex market, where bets affect the fourth decimal of the exchange rate. Not at any time, but there are periods of volatility where 5 minutes counts. Of course, this speculation also has an associated risk: if the direction of change is not precise and it takes an opposite direction, then in the same 5 minutes all the money can be lost.

It is abundantly clear that all of the above factors are decisive in the choice of investment strategy. In the next section, we will demonstrate that we can encounter easily recognizable volatility indicators (charts) as well for general sentiment. For these aspects, technical analysis is applied.

References

Brooks, A. (2011). *Trading price action trends: Technical analysis of price charts bar by bar for the time series trader.* Wiley Trading, Wiley.

Chen, J. (2010). *Essential of technical analyses for financial markets.* John Wiley Sons, Inc.

Di Lorenzo, R. (2013). *Basic technical analysis of the financial market.* Springer.

Dumiter, F., & Turcaş, F. (2022). Theoretical and empirical underpinnings regarding stock market forecasts and predictions. *Studia Universitatis Vasile Goldiş Arad-Economics Series, 32*(1), 1–19.

Greenblatt, J. (2013). *Breakthrough strategies for predicting any market. Second edition. Charting Elliot wave, Lucas, Fibonacci, Gann and time for profit*. Wiley.

Jimon, ŞA., Dumiter, F. C., & Balteş, N. (2021). *Financial sustainability of pension systems: Empirical evidence from Central and Eastern European countries*. Springer.

Linton, D. (2010). *Cloud charts: Trading success with the Ichimoku technique*. Green-On, Tunbridge Wells, England.

Murphy, J. J. (1999). *Technical analysis on the financial markets: A comprehensive guide to trading methods and applications*. New York Institute of Finance.

Patel, M. (2010). *Trading with Ichimoku Clouds: The essential guide to Ichimoku Kinko Hyo technical analysis*. John Wiley and Sons Inc.

Thomsett, M. (2012a). *Technical analysis of stock trends explained: An easy-to-understand system for trading successfully*. Ethan Hathaway Co Ltd.

Thomsett, M. (2012b). *Candlestick charting: Bloomberg visual guide*. John Wiley and Sons Inc.

Tsinaslanidis, P. E., & Zapranis, A. D. (2016). *Technical analysis for algorithmic pattern recognition*. Springer.

Turcaş, F., Dumiter, F., Braica, A., Brezeanu, P., & Opreţ, A. (2016). Using technical analysis for portfolio selection and post-investment analysis. *Economic Computation and Economic Cybernetics Studies and Research, 50*(1), 197–214.

Turcaş, F., Dumiter, F., Brezeanu, P., Fărcaş, P., & Coroiu, S. (2017). Practical aspects of portfolio selection and optimisation on the capital market. *Economic Research-Ekonomska Istrazivanja, 30*(1), 14–30.

CHAPTER 2

Fundamental Analysis *versus* Technical Analysis

Abstract The main areas related to the capital market are represented by: the valuation of financial instruments, stock market theories, portfolio theory, and statistics. We consider it important to answer the question: "what should we know to invest in the capital market?" We should know how to evaluate the company, to see if the market is under-, equi-, or over-evaluated. We will review the main approaches in valuation and show that the value of the issuer (the company as a whole) differs from its stock market capitalization (number of shares or stock price). The whole is not equal to the sum of its components. We will have to refine our financial analysis. The quotation undoubtedly depends on the results of the issuer. But what do we use from the multitude of balance sheet indicators, results, cash flow, rates, and scores? We will briefly present them and highlight their role. We should know how to read periodic reports, and audits, do short due diligence; practically, and make a complete and coherent analysis of the company. Portfolio theories would help us select the securities that best respond to the reward-risk dichotomy. We will see that they are closer to technical analysis than to other areas. Here, too, statistics is needed: we will present it, as much as is strictly necessary, including fractal theories (long tails). Behavioral analysis should also be mentioned. We will not insist on it, but we will specify that the herd effect occurs both in exuberant increases and in stock market crashes. And, no matter how irrational, we must live by following sentiment indicators. Finally, our analysis must consider the following questions: Is there

F. C. Dumiter and F. M. Turcaş, *Technical Analysis Applications*,
https://doi.org/10.1007/978-3-031-27416-9_2

a direct correlation between the company's results and the stock market evolution? What does the correlation mean and how can we use it for portfolio selection? What are market multipliers? How can the discounts used in the valuation be explained? What about primes and synergies? What is market manipulation? How do we recognize important events on the chart and how do we relate to them? What are corrected charts? These are questions that we will show how to look for the answer to.

Keywords Financial instruments · Capital market · Valuation · Portfolio Theories · Behavioral analysis

2.1 Modern Portfolio Theory: Return-Risk

"*Don't put all your eggs in one basket*" is an idiom, including for stocks: if you drop the basket, all is lost (Fabozzi & Pachamanova, 2016). Similarly, if all resources are invested in a single security, the occurrence of any single negative event (materialization of a specific risk) can have disastrous effects on the entire investment.

Catastrophic events can strike investors at any time: stock market crises, calamities, and wars—these are systemic risks, against which it is difficult to elaborate defenses. The COVID-19 pandemic, the Russian-Ukrainian war, and the container, chip, or energy crisis are examples of events that have triggered recent, unpredictable crises with devastating effects on stock market investors because they have affected the vast majority of listed securities. These are systemic risks, and avoiding them is not always possible; they are also difficult to counteract or require significant costs (arbitrage, insurance, etc.) (Fig. 2.1).

But there are specific risks, such as loss of key people in the firm, theft, ill-considered management decisions, and miscarriages of justice. To mitigate the effect of these individual events, portfolio theories have been developed. For example, the bankruptcy of one company is a specific event and one that generally does not affect other companies in the portfolio (Those who experienced the effects of the Lehman Brothers bankruptcy may disagree with us—and they are right!). For such situations, it is useful to diversify the portfolio: if you had not one but three similar companies, the effects of the insolvency of one of them would be softened (Fig. 2.2).

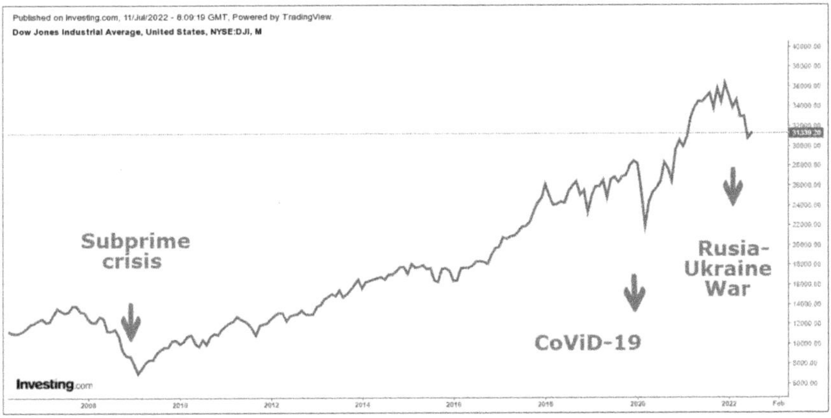

Fig. 2.1 Systemic risks—Stock market crisis (*Source* investing.com)

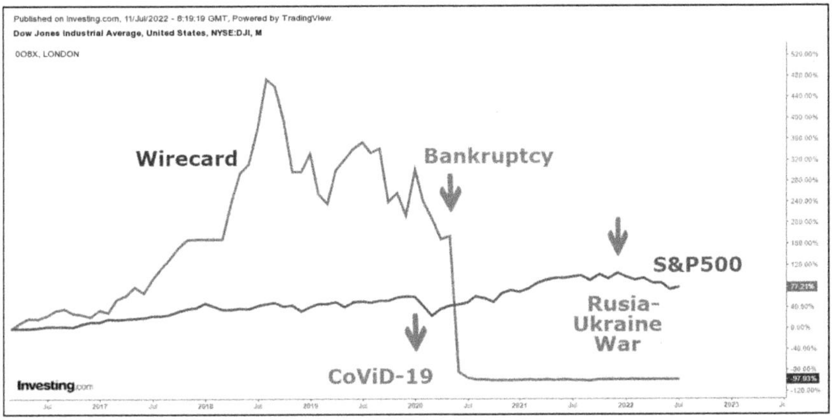

Fig. 2.2 Specific risk—Bankruptcy (*Source* investing.com)

The first important consequence is the need to diversify in order to disperse non-systemic risk. The first notable attempt was Benjamin Graham's landmark 1949 book The Intelligent Investor (Graham, 1949). With few asset classes available, the author proposed a distribution between stocks and bonds that varied according to market movements.

In the 1950s, Markowitz laid the groundwork for modern portfolio theory, in which he proposed a model of minimizing risk for a given return (or vice versa: maximizing return for an accepted level of risk).

In fact, by default, this approach validates the basics of technical analysis: it is based only on the issuer's share price and does not take into account the elements of fundamental analysis at all.

This approach is based on Famma's principle of market information efficiency: the share price in efficient markets incorporates all available information about the issuer and is therefore sufficient to fully characterize the value of the company. Obviously, this assertion is far from the truth in practice: in fact, the company's financial data determine the stock market price. This avoids the Grossman-Stiglitz stock market paradox: if the markets were perfectly informationally efficient, no profit could be made from analyzing the company; but if nobody analyzed the company, how would we know whether the share price is correct in relation to the reality in the company?

The second premise is to consider the parameters necessary to define the characteristics of the portfolio: return and risk. In the MPT version, these are represented by the statistical mean and the root mean square deviation of the daily changes in securities (Elton et al., 2014).

The mathematical rationale for using the two parameters in security valuation, mean μ and dispersion σ, comes from the fact that they uniquely define the normal (Gaussian) statistical distribution (Kroese & Chan, 2014), in the form of the probability density function:

$$F(x) = \frac{1}{\sigma\sqrt{2\pi}} e^{-\frac{1}{2}\left(\frac{x-\mu}{\sigma}\right)^2} \tag{2.1}$$

thus being necessary and sufficient for the construction of the mathematical model.

Therefore, two notions are fundamental in the process of selecting and valuing shares in the capital market: the estimated profit (return) and the risk taken.

In general, the return is defined as a ratio: what percent of the amount invested is estimated to be earned at the end of the holding period.

As a formula, the annual percentage yield r_a for an initial investment S_0 and a final S_f result is:

$$r_a = \frac{(S_f - S_i)}{S_i} \tag{2.2}$$

where profit/loss ($S_f - S_i$) includes all the benefits acquired from holding the shares during one year: increase/decrease in value, dividends received or promised, benefits of shareholders, interest on the loan of securities, etc., but also all costs related to the investment: commissions, taxes, fees, and deductions.

Because investments are rarely held for a full year without further transactions, the annualized rate for an investment held for n days is calculated on the compound interest principle:

$$r_a = \left(\frac{S_f}{S_i}\right)^{\frac{365}{n}} - 1 \tag{2.3}$$

The formula seems simple, but in the investment process, there are often multiple maneuvers in a certain period: withdrawals/cash contributions, granting of free shares (allocated or not allocated in the reference period), changes in the investment position (partial sales, sequential inflows on purchase, execution of orders at various price levels), corporate operations with effects on the value of the portfolio (consolidations/splits of the nominal value, the issuance of free shares on account of dividends, etc.), and adjustment of the value of structured products or derivatives. To deal with these variables, the annual rate of return can be calculated using money-weighted and time-weighted methods.

The GIPS standards provide specific procedures for assessing returns on complex portfolios.

The percentage yield is easy to understand, has a unanimously known meaning in the economic environment, and is useful in calculating the return on the portfolio (when several investment products are held):

$$r_{\text{total}} = \sum r_k \cdot p_k \tag{2.4}$$

where p_k represents the value weight of the title k in the portfolio.

The deficiency of this type of return is that it cannot be summed up: the sum of the yields over different periods is not equal to the total yield. If today the value of the holding decreases by 50%, tomorrow a 100% increase is needed to compensate for it (to reach a zero overall result).

However, at low values of daily profits (below ± 3%, a threshold rarely exceeded in mature markets) the differences are minor between the sum of daily profits and the total multi-period profit and the two can be assimilated.

The logarithmic yield eliminates the problem of summing up the daily results, but it is not additive above the portfolio: the total yield cannot be obtained by summing up the results of individual securities weighted by the percentage of holding:

$$r_{\log} = \log\left(\frac{S_f}{S_i}\right) = \log(S_f) - \log(S_i) \tag{2.5}$$

Risk is harder to define mathematically.

In Modern Portfolio Theory (MPT), risk is equated with uncertainty. On the face of it, this is a logically sound solution: the less accurately we can intuit the evolution of security, the riskier the investment. Obviously, this assertion does not hold for positive developments (MPT considers any changes, including favorable ones, to be risky)—this shortcoming is remedied by Post-Modern Portfolio Theory, in which only unfavorable changes (e.g., declines in share prices) are treated as risky.

If the distribution is assumed to be normal (Gaussian), risk can be interpreted as the standard deviation from the mean value = the variance.

If the risk is defined by the variance of profitability:

$$\sigma_{T,i} = \sqrt{\frac{\sum \left(\mu_{T,i} - P_{t,i}\right)^2}{T}} \tag{2.6}$$

An example of an efficient frontier calculated for 3 securities listed on the BSE (SIF1, BRD, and SNP) is shown in Fig. 2.3. The points on the curve give the best return for a given risk (variance). The efficient frontier (whose first mathematical equation is deduced by one of the authors of the theory) is constructed with the following initial data, for all securities: return, variance, and covariance (correlation between securities). These must be predicted, not taken from history!

Based on past data, https://www.portfoliovisualizer.com/efficient-frontier#analysisResults effective boundaries can be drawn for portfolios of securities listed on different markets, but also for investments in different areas.

Let's explain the results with a concrete example. Figure 2.4 shows (blue curve) the efficient frontier calculated on the basis of the means, variance, and correlation between the US stock market, long-term treasury, REIT real estate market, and gold, calculated on historical values from 1994 to summer 2022. Theoretically, any efficient portfolio lies on

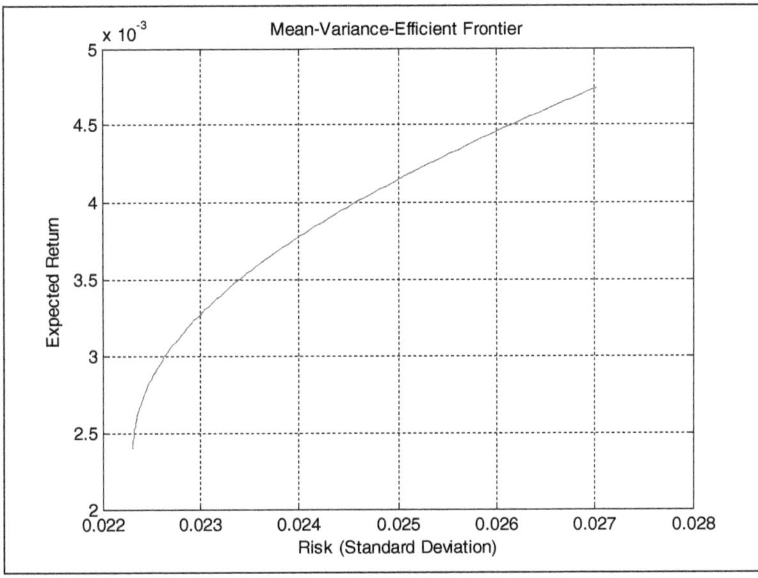

Fig. 2.3 Efficient frontier—part I (*Source* MATLAB calculation)

this curve: depending on the degree of risk assumed (represented on the abscissa = standard deviation), the weighting of securities is chosen so that the portfolio lies on the curve.

The chart in Fig. 2.5 helps us in selecting securities.

The tangent to the graph that passes through the return on risk-free assets (zero abscissae: e.g., government securities) determines the Sharpe portfolio, the most sought-after by investors (Fig. 2.6).

Two elements should be highlighted:

1. The portfolio should be built on future, forecasted data and not on historical data. Returns can be estimated well, the risk is harder to estimate and correlation between assets is almost impossible to estimate rationally.
2. Theory suggests that risk is directly proportional to return: the higher the expected return, the higher the risk. Broadly speaking, this assertion is true: bank deposits are safe, but usually don't even cover inflation; stocks are riskier, but offer higher returns; Forex

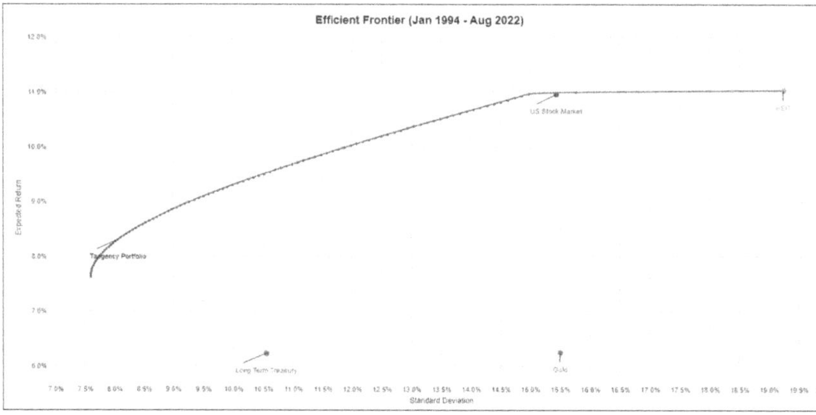

Fig. 2.4 Efficient frontier—part II (*Source* Own processing)

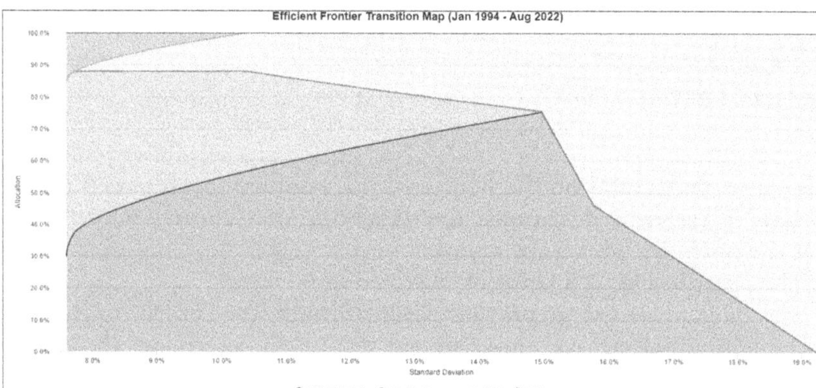

Fig. 2.5 Weight of securities in the efficient frontier (*Source* Own processing)

promises huge winnings at equally huge risks. But this is not exactly true of the stock market (see Table 2.1), DJIA components are ordered by volatility, and it is obvious that the order only coincides roughly with the reverse order of stock market performance.

What does this have to do with technical analysis? Well, return and risk (variance) can best be visualized on the chart of the security, i.e., on the

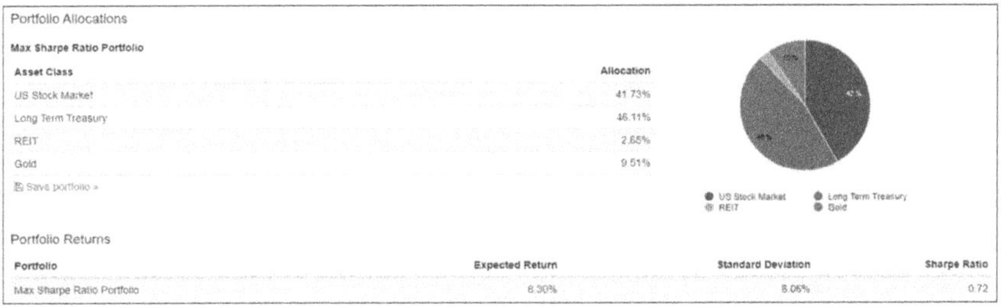

Portfolio Allocations

Max Sharpe Ratio Portfolio

Asset Class	Allocation
US Stock Market	41.73%
Long Term Treasury	46.11%
REIT	2.65%
Gold	9.51%

Save portfolio »

Portfolio Returns

Portfolio	Expected Return	Standard Deviation	Sharpe Ratio
Max Sharpe Ratio Portfolio	8.30%	8.06%	0.72

Fig. 2.6 Sharpe portfolio (*Source* Own processing)

Table 2.1 DJIA companies return-risk 1-year data

Company	Perf Year	▾ Volatility W
NIKE, Inc.	-39.40%	4.06%
The Boeing Company	-41.24%	3.79%
Salesforce, Inc.	-43.52%	3.36%
Intel Corporation	-49.65%	3.34%
Caterpillar Inc.	-6.80%	2.91%
The Walt Disney Company	-42.99%	2.87%
JPMorgan Chase & Co.	-36.02%	2.74%
Apple Inc.	2.42%	2.72%
Chevron Corporation	53.84%	2.71%
American Express Company	-17.89%	2.69%
The Goldman Sachs Group, Inc.	-21.49%	2.68%
Verizon Communications Inc.	-30.61%	2.64%
Walgreens Boots Alliance, Inc.	-31.25%	2.64%
3M Company	-37.71%	2.62%
Microsoft Corporation	-15.80%	2.58%
Honeywell International Inc.	-19.28%	2.57%
Visa Inc.	-18.07%	2.54%
International Business Machines Corporation	-10.11%	2.53%
Dow Inc.	-20.36%	2.29%
The Travelers Companies, Inc.	2.64%	2.21%

Source finwiz.com

Bollinger bands (which are plotted at ± 2 mean squared deviations from the moving averages.

2.2 Securities Correlation

An interesting problem arises when it comes to asset correlation.

Financial markets, especially in today's era of globalization and free movement of capital, are increasingly interlinked globally and asset prices are increasingly dependent on the macroeconomic context in which they operate. Stock markets move in tandem, as Fig. 2.7 makes clear.

Markets of different types are also correlated with each other, as intermarket studies show. For example, stocks and bonds are positively correlated (vary in the same direction) and inversely correlated with commodities (vary in the opposite direction). At least in theory, because in practice it is not happened always (Fig. 2.8).

Modern Portfolio Theory suggests building investments on the principle of arbitrage: buying securities that vary as opposite as possible so that declines in some securities are offset by possible increases in others. It may be a sound policy to mitigate losses and risks, but the stock market is meant to increase shareholder wealth, not preserve it.

The mathematical theory does not distinguish between 2 perfectly correlated securities with the same return risk. On the contrary: investors would look for such securities, for at least 2 reasons: (1) they would only

Fig. 2.7 Correlation between international stock markets (*Source* investing.com)

Fig. 2.8 Intermarket correlations (*Source* investing.com)

have to track/know one issuer and could react on both issuers simultaneously and 92) they could thus protect themselves from non-systematic (specific/accidental) risks at one issuer because these do not recur at the other.

Let's look at the correlation between copper and zinc quotes—a nearly perfect positive correlation (Fig. 2.9). The explanation here is immediate: copper-zinc alloy is brass, a raw material with remarkably many civil uses. Equally clear are the correlations between raw materials and direct processors (Fig. 2.10). Companies that are only concerned with operating existing assets (cow in the Boston Consulting diagram) have an almost identical and direct variation with raw material. In Fig. 2.11, we have depicted two relatively small companies SNP listed on the Bucharest Stock Exchange and OMV listed on the Vienna Stock Exchange, whose only concern is the primary processing of hydrocarbons. Companies with high value-added also have the same variation as raw materials, but β (covariance with the base stock) almost double (Fig. 2.10).

But think how useful it would be to find a significant correlation, positive or negative, between theoretically economically uncorrelated assets: we would only need to study one stock and we would have an insight into how the other would behave. And if there was a temporary gap, the situation would be perfect: we could predict the reaction of the second one just from the variation of the first one.

Fig. 2.9 Copper-zinc correlation (*Source* investing.com)

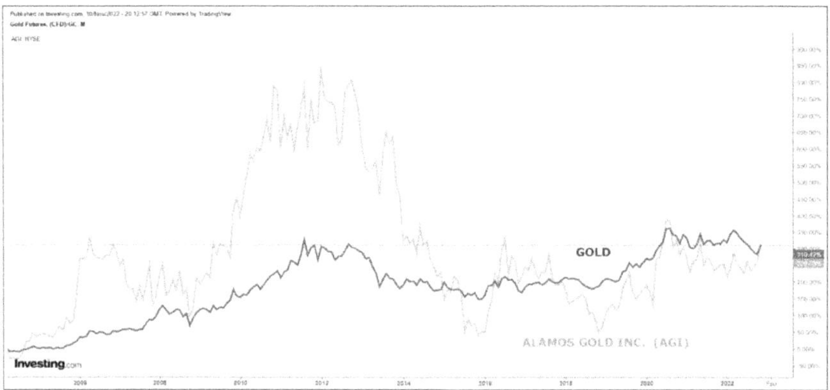

Fig. 2.10 Raw material vs. processor correlation (*Source* investing.com)

2.3 Market Multipliers

Technical analysis is based on the past performance of the stock and tries to predict the next move. But it cannot be used on its own—however vehement its advocates may be, without a minimum of fundamental analysis, technical analysis cannot survive. While it can explain whether an upswing or a correction is coming, technical analysis alone cannot justify why the price is \$10/share and not \$1 or \$100/share.

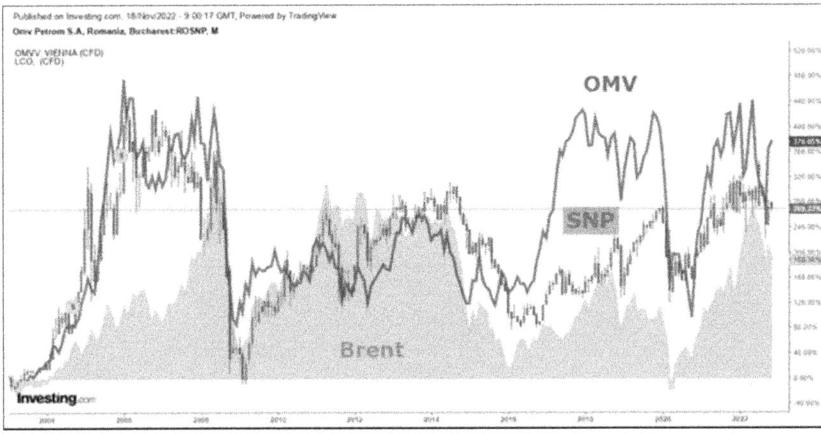

Fig. 2.11 Brent oil vs. processor correlation (*Source* investing.com)

So fundamental analysis is necessary. But which indicators are the determinants of pricing? Table 2.2 shows some fundamental and technical indicators as they are presented free on analysis and trading sites, analysts' opinions, and media news. As you can see, it is not the abundance of data or the calculation of indicators that is the problem, but their interpretation. How can 100 financial indicators, another 100 technical ones, the daily news and rumors—how can they all be condensed into a single parameter: the share price?

Here's a look at how many annual, half-yearly and quarterly financial statements Bloomberg presents for listed companies worldwide (Fig. 2.12).

Obviously, a selection has to be made: what is important, what are market participants looking for, and what can investors look for in the thousands of companies that can be selected in the portfolio?

The market valuation is recommended by the International Valuation Standards (IVS, 2022): *«The market approach often uses market multiples derived from a set of comparables, each with different multiples. The selection of the appropriate multiple within the range requires judgment, considering qualitative and quantitative factors.»*

But multipliers are also numerous (Table 2.3):

Indicators vary widely across companies listed on major stock exchanges (Fig. 2.13).

Table 2.2 Some indicators presented at AAPL issuer, analyst views, and market news

Index	DJIA S&P500	P/E	23.93	EPS (ttm)	6.05	Insider Own	0.07%	Shs Outstand	16.16B	Perf Week	6.98%
Market Cap	2265.74B	Forward P/E	22.47	EPS next Y	6.44	Insider Trans	-4.41%	Shs Float	16.06B	Perf Month	-3.36%
Income	99.63B	PEG	2.69	EPS next Q	1.27	Inst Own	59.70%	Short Float	0.68%	Perf Quarter	10.90%
Sales	387.54B	P/S	5.85	EPS this Y	71.40%	Inst Trans	-0.05%	Short Ratio	1.31	Perf Half Y	11.51%
Book/sh	3.60	P/B	40.22	EPS next Y	5.55%	ROA	28.10%	Target Price	183.54	Perf Year	2.72%
Cash/sh	3.08	P/C	46.98	EPS next 5Y	8.93%	ROE	153.00%	52W Range	129.04 - 182.94	Perf YTD	-18.45%
Dividend	0.92	P/FCF	24.41	EPS past 5Y	22.00%	ROI	58.00%	52W High	-14.90%	Beta	1.25
Dividend %	0.64%	Quick Ratio	0.80	Sales past 5Y	11.10%	Gross Margin	43.30%	52W Low	20.64%	ATR	4.69
Employees	154000	Current Ratio	0.90	Sales Q/Q	1.90%	Oper. Margin	30.50%	RSI (14)	59.49	Volatility	2.94% 3.04%
Optionable	Yes	Debt/Eq	2.06	EPS Q/Q	-7.70%	Profit Margin	25.70%	Rel Volume	2.67	Prev Close	144.80
Shortable	Yes	LT Debt/Eq	1.63	Earnings	Oct 27 AMC	Payout	14.60%	Avg Volume	82.83M	Price	155.68
Recom	1.90	SMA20	8.30%	SMA50	2.31%	SMA200	-0.74%	Volume	84,396,943	Change	7.51%

Oct-28-22	**Reiterated**	Wedbush	Outperform	$220 → $200
Oct-28-22	**Reiterated**	Robert W. Baird	Outperform	$185 → $170
Oct-28-22	**Reiterated**	KeyBanc Capital Markets	Overweight	$185 → $177
Oct-28-22	**Reiterated**	Deutsche Bank	Buy	$175 → $170
Oct-28-22	**Reiterated**	DA Davidson	Buy	$185 → $167
Oct-28-22	**Reiterated**	Credit Suisse	Outperform	$190 → $184
Oct-28-22	**Reiterated**	Citigroup	Buy	$185 → $175
Oct-28-22	**Reiterated**	Barclays	Equal Weight	$155 → $156
Oct-17-22	**Reiterated**	Morgan Stanley	Overweight	$180 → $177
Oct-13-22	**Reiterated**	Credit Suisse	Outperform	$201 → $190
Oct-11-22	**Reiterated**	Barclays	Equal Weight	$169 → $155
Sep-29-22	**Upgrade**	Rosenblatt	Neutral → Buy	$160 → $189
Sep-29-22	**Downgrade**	BofA Securities	Buy → Neutral	$185 → $160
Aug-17-22	**Upgrade**	Credit Suisse	Neutral → Outperform	$201
Jul-26-22	**Initiated**	Itau BBA	Underperform	$136
Jul-20-22	**Reiterated**	Wells Fargo	Overweight	$205 → $185
Jul-20-22	**Reiterated**	Morgan Stanley	Overweight	$185 → $180
Jul-06-22	**Reiterated**	Goldman	Neutral	$157 → $130
Jun-28-22	**Reiterated**	Evercore ISI	Outperform	$210 → $180
May-25-22	**Reiterated**	Loop Capital	Buy	$210 → $180

Oct-28-22	11:37AM	Apple stock surges toward best day since 2020 as its dubbed rare bright spot amid Big Tech carnage MarketWatch
	11:34AM	Apple has balanced iPhone pricing and volume fairly well, analyst says Yahoo Finance Video
	11:32AM	Apple Dodges Tech Rout, Even While Warning of Holiday Slowdown Bloomberg
	11:28AM	Apple caters to those who want a premium experience, analyst says Yahoo Finance Video
	11:27AM	Apple Warns Of Holiday Sales Slowdown, Forecasts Big Drop In Mac Business Investor's Business Daily
	11:15AM	Apple Is the Only Big Tech Consolation in Wild $477 Billion Rout Bloomberg
	11:15AM	Apple Escapes the Tech Carnage: Here's What Traders Should Watch for Now TheStreet.com
	10:46AM	Stock Market Ignores Tech Wreck; Amazon Shattered But Apple Higher Investor's Business Daily
	10:38AM	US STOCKS-Wall Street rises as Apple boost outweighs Amazon gloom Reuters
	10:28AM	Apple's Steady Results Prove Why It's the Ultimate Warren Buffett Stock Motley Fool
	10:08AM	Exclusive: Construction could happen soon at Apple in RTP American City Business Journals
	10:06AM	Tech Boom Ends as Companies From Amazon to Meta Adjust to Turbulent Times The Wall Street Journal
	10:05AM	Dow Jones Rallies On Key Inflation Data; Amazon Dives, Apple Climbs On Earnings Investor's Business Daily
	10:02AM	One Year On, Metaverse Frenzy Yet to Yield Dividends Bloomberg
	09:49AM	Apple is now worth 9x more than Meta Yahoo Finance Video
	09:48AM	S&P 500 consolidates gains, mega-cap tech stocks lead Yahoo Finance Video
	09:39AM	Stocks mixed at open, Apple gains, Amazon extends losses Yahoo Finance Video
	09:25AM	Apple delivers record revenue even as iPhone sales were lighter than expected Yahoo Finance Video
	08:21AM	Dow Jones Futures: Apple Holds, Amazon Joins Megacap Meltdown; What To Do Now Investor's Business Daily
	08:11AM	US STOCKS-Futures retreat as warnings from Amazon, Apple fan recession fears Reuters
	08:05AM	7 Must-See Metrics Highlight Apple's Record Fiscal Fourth Quarter Motley Fool
	07:58AM	ECB Tones It Down, GDP Intrigue, Old-School Stocks Rule, Amazon in Depth TheStreet.com
	06:34AM	Apple Is the Winner of a Gruesome Earnings Season. Maybe Buffett Was Right. Barrons.com
	06:17AM	Apple Stock Higher On Q4 Earnings Beat, Hopeful Holiday Sales Forecast TheStreet.com
	06:05AM	Did Apple Just Stick a Pin in the Google-Facebook Duopoly? Motley Fool
	06:00AM	Apple offers a dim light in an otherwise 'dark earnings season': Morning Brief Yahoo Finance
	05:41AM	With Talk of a Recession Brewing, Here's How Investors Can Prepare to Ride Out the Storm Motley Fool
	05:34AM	Futures sink as grim forecasts from Amazon, Apple fan recession fears Reuters

Source finviz.com

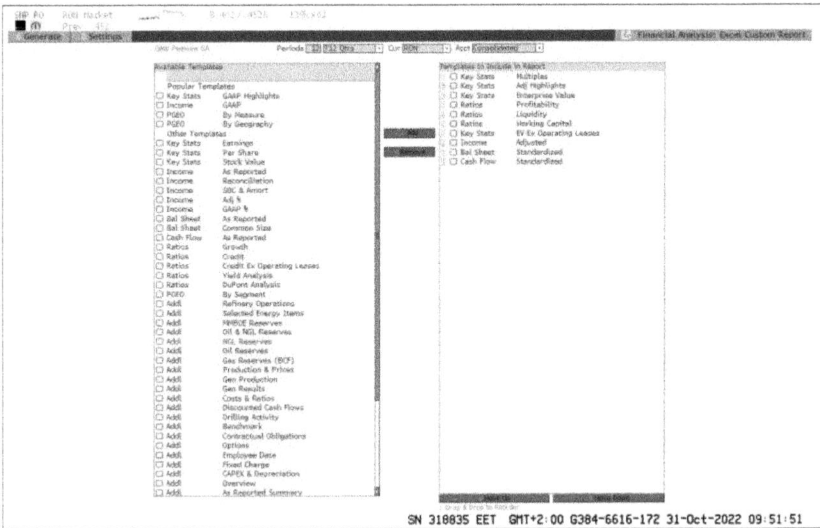

Fig. 2.12 Bloomberg screen for generating the Excel (or.pdf) financial analysis file (*Source* Own processing)

Table 2.3 Multipliers and stock market indicators calculated by Damodaran

Multiples	PE Ratios, PEG Ratios and Expected Growth Rates by Industry Sector	1. U.S. 2. Europe 3. Japan 4. Emerg Mkt 5. China 6. India 7. Global	This lists out the PE ratio, expected growth (Value Line) and the PE/growth by industry group for the most recent time period.	
	Price and Value to Book Ratios and ROE by Industry Sector	1. U.S. 2. Europe 3. Japan 4. Emerg Mkt 1. China 2. India 5. Global	This lists outs Price/Book value ratios and ROE by industry group for the most recent time period.	
	Price and Value to Sales Ratios and Margins by Industry Sector	1. U.S. 2. Europe 3. Japan 4. Emerg Mkt 1. China 2. India 5. Global	This lists out Price/Sales ratios and margins by industry group for the most recent time period.	
	Value/EBIT & Value/EBITDA Multiples by Industry Sector	1. U.S. 2. Europe 3. Japan 4. Emerg Mkt 1. China 2. India 5. Global	This lists out Enterprise Value / EBITDA by industry group for the most recent time period. Enterprise Value is the market value of equity plus the book value of debt minus cash.	
	Multiples by Market Cap Class (US)	Download	The averages for key equity and enterprise value multiples are reported for firms in different market cap classes in the U.S.	
	Earnings, Book Value and Sales Multiple Averages by Country	Download	This lists out the average PE, Price to book, Price to Sales and Enterprise Value multiples by country. It also includes summary statistics on returns on equity and capital and margins (net and operating).	
	Market Regressions of Multiples against fundamentals		This lists the output from the latest regressions across the entire market of multiples against fundamentals (PE, PBV, PS, EV Multiples).	

Source https://pages.stern.nyu.edu/~adamodar/New_Home_Page/datacurrent.html

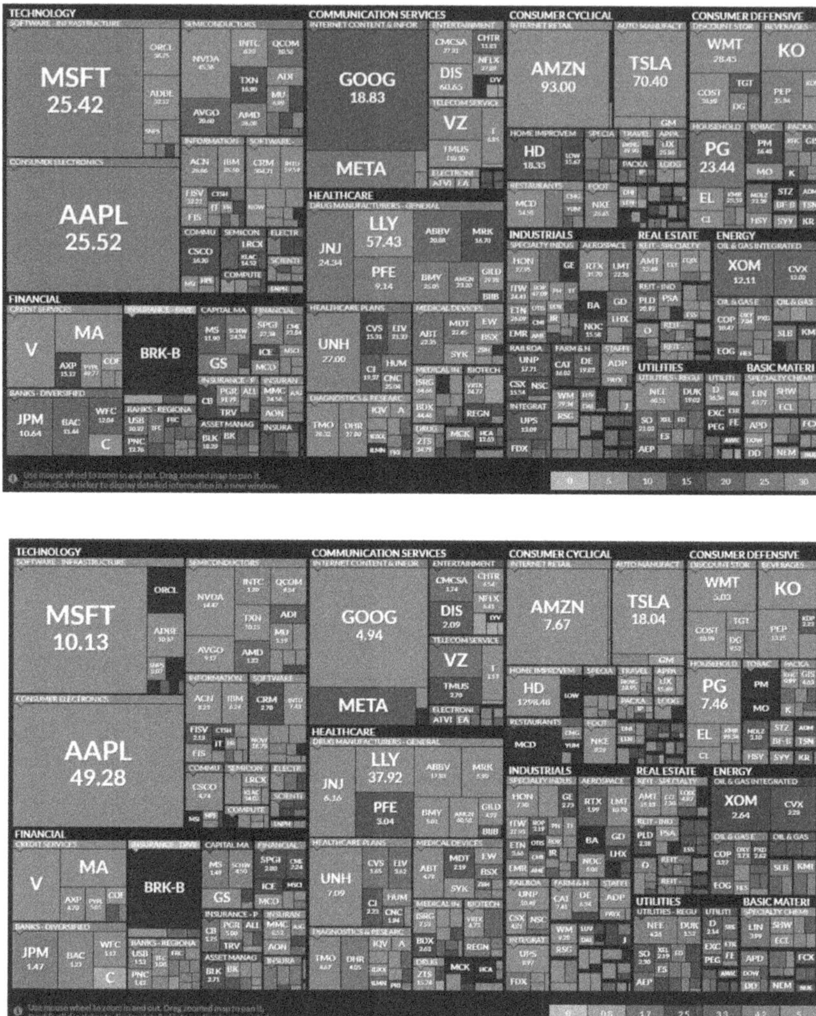

Fig. 2.13 P/E and P/BV across S&P500 companies (*Source* https://finviz.com/map.ashx?st=pb)

The main multipliers are:

$$P/E = \text{Price Earning Ratio} = \frac{\text{Price}}{\text{Earning per share}} = \frac{\text{Market capitalisation}}{\text{Net profit}} \tag{2.7}$$

$$\text{PBV} = \text{Price per Book Value} = \frac{\text{Price}}{\text{Unit Value of Net Assets}} = \frac{\text{Market Capitalisation}}{\text{Book Value of Equity}} \tag{2.8}$$

$$\text{DV} = \text{Dividend Yield} = \frac{\text{Dividend per share}}{\text{Price}} \tag{2.9}$$

However, comparable multipliers that do not take into account share prices should also be considered, the most popular being $\frac{\text{EV}}{\text{EBIT(DA)}}$, $\frac{\text{EV}}{\text{Cash Flow}}$, $\frac{\text{Sales}}{\text{EV}}$ (where EV is Enterprise Value = market value of equity + value of interest-bearing debt – minus any cash on hand, including surplus assets, to cover it).

It should be pointed out that the indicators might be divergent. Companies with good P/E may have weak P/BV; DY—also important to speculators—varies widely, sometimes causing modest companies to become attractive (Table 2.4).

Although they seem easy to determine (they are listed in all markets) and easy to use (simple mathematical relationships, which you can easily find with a simple web search), indicators and multipliers have a major shortcoming: they vary widely depending on the state of the market because nobody knows what a rational value for them would be. In fact, at times of strong market momentum, market trends have a greater weight on the value of shares than the actual performance of the company. Given the fluctuations of the main stock market indicators of the Bucharest Stock Exchange (BVB), we infer that the influence of market conditions (not directly related to the issuer) is decisive in determining the price, being more significant than the influence of the issuer's results (Table 2.5).

Table 2.4 Romanian market indicators

Symbol	ISIN	Market Capitalization	Book Value	Book Value Date	PBV	PER	PER Date	DIVY	Dividend Year	Type
EBS	AT0000652011	53,080,300,000								I
SNP	ROSNPPACNOR9	25,603,136,967	36,908,390,000	6/30/2022	0.69	3.92	6/30/2022	9.96	2022	C
SNG	ROSNGNACNOR3	14,780,949,040	9,276,246,000	6/30/2022	1.59	5.13	6/30/2022	9.91	2021	C
SNN	ROSNNEACNOR8	12,126,084,539	8,988,330,864	6/30/2022	1.35	6.48	6/30/2022	4.91	2021	C
TLV	ROTLVAACNOR1	12,030,189,961	9,976,198,000	6/30/2022	1.21	5.85	6/30/2022	6.65	2021	C
FP	ROFPTAACNOR5	11,067,728,879	16,327,278,336	6/30/2022	0.68	1.51	6/30/2022	7.02	2021	I
BRD	ROBRDBACNOR2	7,874,987,153	5,971,459,000	6/30/2022	1.32	6.01	6/30/2022	11.37	2021	C
CRC	ROCHOBACNOR8	5,549,322,888	854,888,969	12/31/2021	6.49	11.46	12/31/2021	0.72	2022	C
ONE	ROJ8YZPDHWW8	3,421,404,374	2,121,178,433	6/30/2022	1.61	4.82	6/30/2022	1.06	2022	C
DIGI	NL0012294474	3,060,000,000						2.64	2021	I
TGN	ROTGNTACNOR8	2,655,001,822	3,882,719,364	6/30/2022	0.68	12.03	6/30/2022	6.57	2021	C
EL	ROELECACNOR5	2,255,347,816	4,633,206,000	6/30/2022	0.49	-4.97	6/30/2022	6.77	2021	C
M	ROMEDLACNOR6	2,176,418,659	432,255,373	6/30/2022	5.04	25.01	6/30/2022			C
RRC	ROPTRMACNOR5	1,991,940,429	2,079,472,561	6/30/2022	0.96	-4.48	6/30/2022	0.00	2008	C
SCD	ROSCDBACNOR8	1,421,914,762	922,556,750	6/30/2022	1.54	13.81	6/30/2022	4.57	2016	I
TEL	ROTSELACNOR9	1,275,474,671	3,423,022,000	6/30/2022	0.37	-19.54	6/30/2022	5.00	2020	C
SIF1	ROSIFAACNOR2	1,262,784,789	3,164,199,736	6/30/2022	0.40	6.92	6/30/2022	2.41	2021	I
EVER	ROSIFBACNOR0	1,216,618,294	2,278,229,067	6/30/2022	0.53	23.53	6/30/2022	5.12	2021	I
ARS	ROAEROACNOR5	1,119,239,258	445,679,111	6/30/2022	2.51	15.38	6/30/2022	2.04	2021	I
TRP	ROTRPLACNOR7	1,115,648,183	309,587,063	6/30/2022	3.60	5.09	6/30/2022	23.24	2021	C

Showing 1 to 20 of 83 entries   Previous 1 2 3 4 5 Next

Source https://www.bvb.ro/FinancialInstruments/SelectedData/Indicators

Table 2.5 Values of stock market indicators

Date	*P/E*	*P/BV*	*DY*
31.07.2007	22,38	3,30	1,99
24.02.2009	2,56	0,49	13,41
09.04.2010	19,71	1,42	2,06
May 2020	6,70	0,89	6,74

Source Date from BSE

2.4 Discounted Cash Flow Forecasts

DCF is a valuation method whereby cash flows are converted into value via the capitalization rate (cost of capital). The IVSC standards state: «*Under the DCF method the forecasted cash flow is discounted back to the valuation date, resulting in a present value of the asset.*»

The simplified formula is:

$$V = \sum_{i-1}^{n} \frac{FCF_i}{(1+c)^n} \tag{2.10}$$

where V is the value of the firm, FCF_i is the free cash flow available to the investor (which is surplus, not needed for the production process, and can be extracted from the firm), and c is the cost of capital, which is usually taken from the market. The method is applied when a large variation in the firm's activity is expected (for cruising/maturity periods, methods based on earnings multipliers are quicker and more reliable) and may also incorporate a final term (a residual value) to include perpetual activity.

As presented by the standards, the application of the approach is flawed. Suppose an investor has acquired the land, drawn up the project, and obtained the necessary permits to build a block of flats. He will take out a loan to build, build the block in one year and sell it in two years at a substantial profit, pay off the loan and liquidate the SPV. The DCF valuation will give a high value (basically the profit made—time being very short, bank interest, and discount rate have minimal influence). But, at the time of the analysis, all the company has its land (which should be valued at market value—purchase value), maybe a bit more valuable because it has the permit obtained. Considering common values in the Romanian real estate market: land cost = maximum of 20% of the project value; developer's profit = at least 30% of the project value, it clearly results from the logical break in the DCF valuation: the appraiser will now propose the final value of the firm, when, in fact, the actual value is only that of the land.

But all the harm for the good: it is exactly this logical flaw that investors must exploit. The present value is what it is, but in the future, the value will be something else entirely. And hence, the investment decision is simple: is it worth buying the stock now and selling it in the future or not? Perhaps formula (2.7) is too complicated, but its logic may be useful to investors.

2.5 Rational Periods and Periods of Rush/panic

Like any human activity, the stock market is affected by the feelings of the participants, especially when they are strong. Although in mature markets most trading is done by skilled investors and machines (automated trading), it is all governed by criteria imposed, more or less subjectively, by humans. The most relevant are the ranges of excessive exuberance and panic, where herd behavior is most evident. An eloquent example of the Romanian market is BRD (one of the largest banks in Romania, a subsidiary of the Société Generale Group).

In the period before the subprime crisis, the Romanian capital market made substantial progress, with triple-digit annual returns being the order of the day. The stock market price (denoted Price in Fig. 2.14) has a meteoric rise until 2007, exceeding by far the value of the Net Unit Profit (denoted Profit) and the Net Book Value (BV = Book Value). This is followed by the panic triggered by the crisis and the "hard landing", in which the share price falls just below book value—an aberration for a bank. Later, after a few more jumps unjustified by the activity of the issuer, the rate returns to a natural level, with P/E and P/BV indicators normalized for Romanian banks.

How can periods of exuberance/panic be recognized? Some analysts have found on the logarithmic graph that the evolution of listed securities is relatively linear (i.e., the stock market rises exponentially), with small deviations from a straight line. Any significant (lasting) deviation from this straight line can be interpreted as a signal of exceptional evolution (Fig. 2.15).

Fig. 2.14 Rush & panic on BRD (*Source* Own processing)

Fig. 2.15 Exuberance and panic on Wall Street (*Source* investing.com)

2.6 Important Events and Their Evolution

Technical analysis alone cannot explain some price movements. For example, in February 2021 Teraplast SA, the largest polymer processor in Eastern Europe, listed on the BSE under the ticker TRP, announced the sale of its steel division and a substantial profit in Q1 2021: RON 201 million compared to a net profit of RON 6 million in Q1 2020. Naturally, the share price skyrocketed (Fig. 2.16) especially as the issuer announced substantial dividend distributions from the profit. This increase could not have been anticipated on the basis of the technical analysis, as it was due exclusively to fundamental financial considerations, i.e., important market news.

Unnatural price movements allow us to detect market manipulation.

Figure 2.17 shows a comparison between the SIF1 and SIF5, both of which are atypical closed-end funds. The jump recorded by SIF1 on 13.09.2013, a variation of + 12.42% compared to the previous day, is clearly discrepant (Table 2.6).

The whole operation is clarified if we follow Table 2.5. Suspicious transactions on the issuer SIF1: in the pre-close of the market on Friday, 13.09.2013, an order was placed that modified the reference (closing) price, in the sense of a substantial increase. Under these conditions, on Monday 16.09.2013 the DEAL transaction could be carried out at

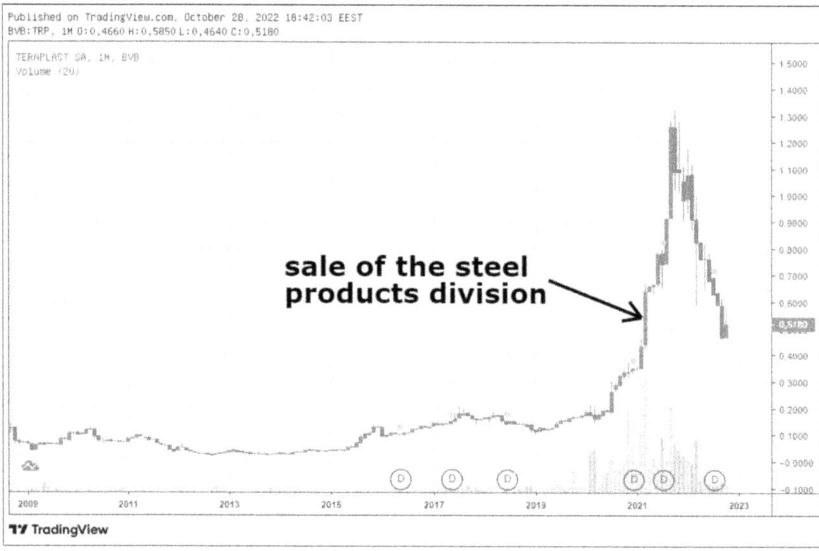

Fig. 2.16 Purely fundamental reasons for the increase (*Source* Own processing)

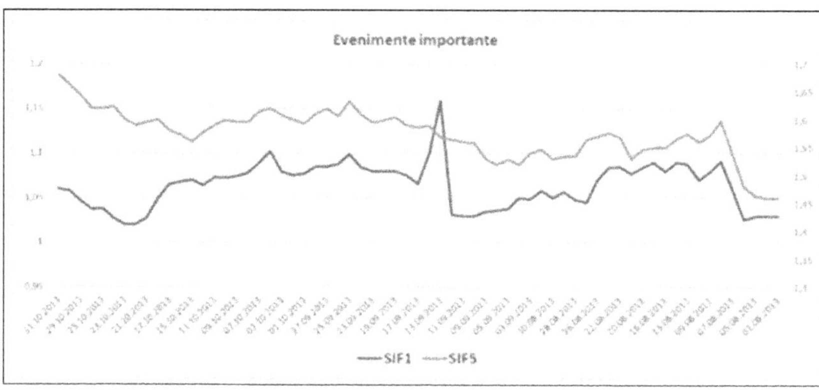

Fig. 2.17 Market manipulation (*Source* Chart plotted in Excel, with data from bvb.ro)

Table 2.6 Market data

Date	*Market*	*Trades*	*Volume*	*Open*	*Min*	*Max*	*Close*	*Var.(%)*
17.09.2013	REGS	208	1,385.500	1,093	1,065	1,093	1,066	−3,09
16.09.2013	REGS	197	490.000	1,11	1,09	1,138	1,1	−5,09
16.09.2013	DEALS	2	34,412.500	1,32	1,32	1,32	1,32	**13,89**
13.09.2013	REGS	316	4,294.000	1,034	1,034	1,159	1,159	**12,42**
12.09.2013	REGS	162	1,326.000	1,032	1,029	1,032	1,031	0,1
11.09.2013	REGS	73	394.500	1,03	1,027	1,035	1,03	0

Source Extract from public data, from the BSE website

another + 13.89%. Without Friday's market manipulation, the DEAL trade would not have been possible at this price, as the issuer has a daily variation limit (price tunnel) of ± 15%.

News (stock market news) can also play a decisive role in the evolution of the price. However, their influence is far less than the issuer and/or the economic press would like it to appear. In Fig. 2.18, it can be seen in a picture from the TGN Half-Yearly Report, where the issuer explains all price changes to economic events that happened in the company. Never mind that you can't read the exact information—neither could we and we didn't get the image from the issuer (although we asked them) at a readable resonance. It is obvious, however, that although they are placed at every minor change, of course, the explanations neither justify the price movements nor help much in predicting the trajectory.

2.7 The Usage of News Sentiment Figures in Constructing Market Sentiment Indices

There is a multitude of indicators that measure stock market sentiment. Quite common is the CNN Business one that measures "fear" and "greed". Based on a scale from 0 to 100, where 0 is extreme fear and 100 is extreme greed, the indicator considers 7 different variables. As of November 18, 2022, here is how the indicator looks like (Fig. 2.19):

The basic premise underlying this indicator is the rationale that too much fear leads to lower stock prices and too much greed has the reverse effect. Seven variables are taken into consideration to calculate this indicator, namely: market momentum, stock price strength, stock price

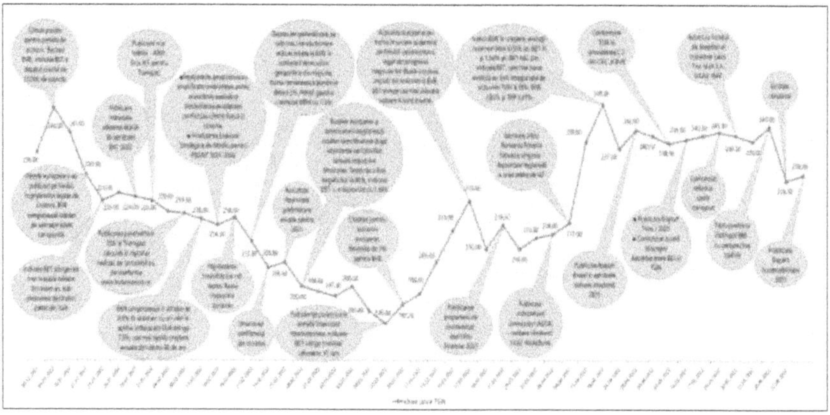

Fig. 2.18 Transgaz's attempt to explain the evolution of the price based on events in the company (*Source* Half-yearly report: https://www.transgaz.ro/sites/default/files/users/user360/Raport%20administratori%20%20Sem.%20I%202022.pdf)

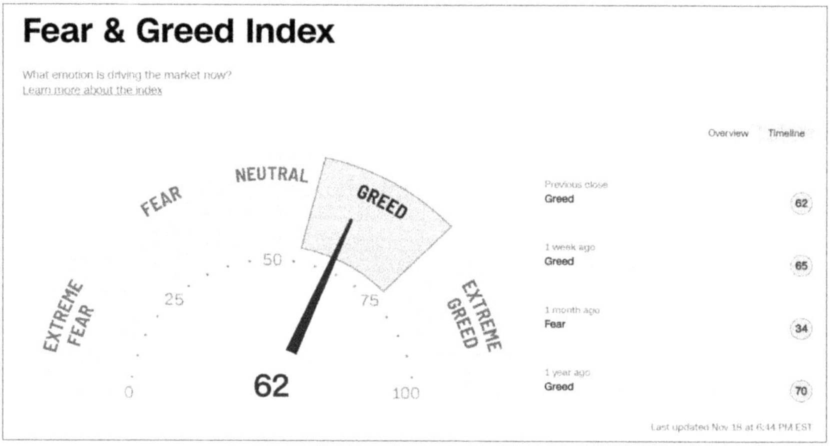

Fig. 2.19 Fear and greed index (*Source* https://edition.cnn.com/markets/fear-and-greed#fng-faq)

breadth, put and call options, market volatility, safe haven demand, and junk bond demand, all weighted equally.

In terms of "testing" this indicator, it is appended the following Fig. 2.20.

Although the correlation is obviously present, we would like to point out that while the "Fear and Greed" indicator (marked blue on the chart) is approaching its highs, the S&P 500 is down **−17,33%** from the all-time high (ATH: **4796.56** vs closing price on November 18th, 2022: **3965.34**).

Moving on, we have tested the VIX, an index that measures volatility in the market. In order to do so, we have overlapped a chart of S&P500 over VIX. Below are our findings (Fig. 2.21):

1. The reverse/inverse correlation tends to be more evident during market downturns, which triggers higher volatility. To prove this point, we have highlighted 2 key moments on the chart (marked as 1 and 2), the first was the 2018 lows and the second was the market sell-off sparked by the coronavirus pandemic.
2. In moments of calm, when the market slowly and surely goes up (Steady Eddie wins the race), the volatility index tends to head down. To highlight this phenomenon, we have flagged moments 3 and 4 on the graph.

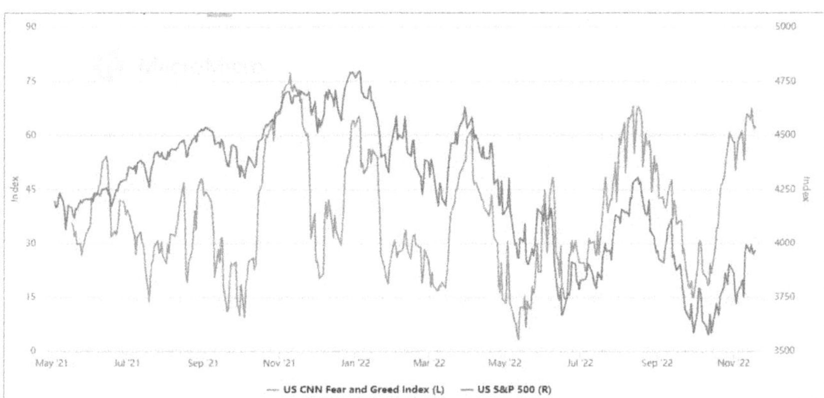

Fig. 2.20 Feer and greed index test (*Source* https://en.macromicro.me/collections/34/us-stock-relative/50108/cnn-fear-and-greed)

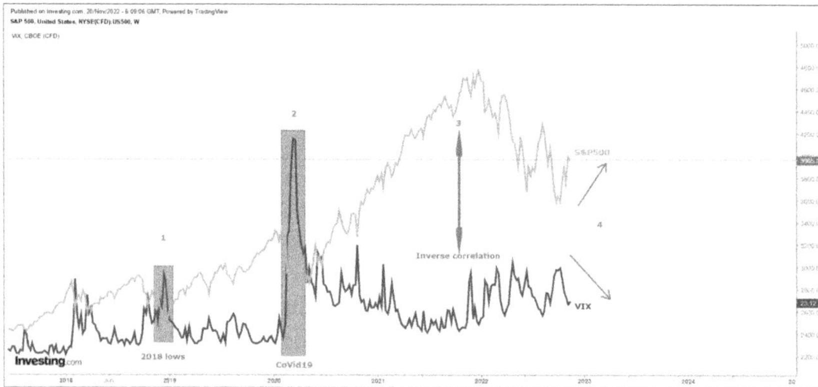

Fig. 2.21 VIX vs. S&P500 (*Source* www.investing.com)

Finally, courtesy of the University of Michigan, which measures the Consumer Sentiment Index and has public data, we compared it to the S&P500 over a 5-year period (Fig. 2.22).

Marked with blue on the chart is the US Index of Consumer Sentiment indicator, which measured from October 2018 (value: 98.6) to the present (value 30 October 2022: 54.7) has fallen by **44.52%** while with orange is the S&P500 (value October 2018: 2,711 vs. October 2022: 3,992) which has risen by **47.25%**.

As the chart attached above shows, our view is that over the medium term, there is no correlation between these 2 benchmarks.

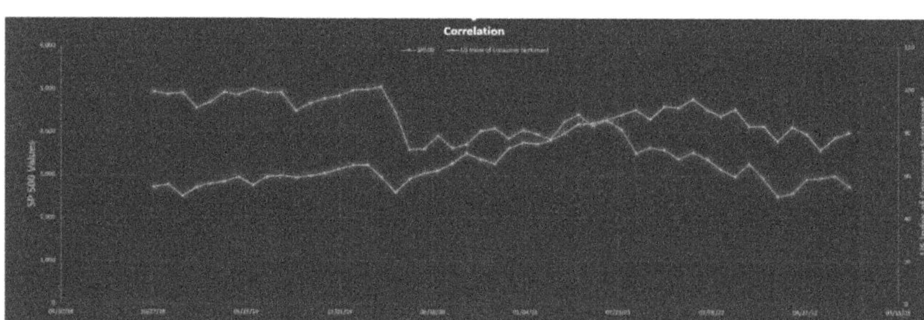

Fig. 2.22 Consumer sentiment vs. S&P500 (*Source* http://www.sca.isr.umich.edu/)

2.8 Finis Coronat Opus

All the efforts of analysts, experts, brokers, traders, investors, and speculators—of all those interested in the stock market—are focused in one direction: trying to predict the future evolution of the stock market price and implicitly to answer the question whether the share price is under-, over- or even-valued and thus to be able to give an opinion as valid as possible: buy, hold, or sell.

The fundamental analysis starts from hundreds of considerations: the general macroeconomic environment, the industry situation and outlook, the positioning of the company in the market, the company's functions and their status, dozens of parameters, and rates deduced from financial reports, compared with similar companies in the industry and the relevant geographical area. Fundamental analysis, however, requires sound economic knowledge, use of mathematics (even if at an elementary level), extensive data research, and especially the interpretation of data, both individually and especially in comparison with other similar companies—perhaps this is why it is not very popular, especially with the general public. But it is certainly used by institutional investors, who benefit from the power of computing technology, which processes huge volumes of data in a short time.

Technical analysis, on the other hand, starts from the information available in the market, of which there are only two; the trading price and the trading volume (quantity). From there, it builds trends, channels, patterns, Japanese formations, dozens of indicators and oscillators, to finally answer the same fundamental questions: overbought or oversold, respectively, buy-hold-sell selection (here, we would add the option of indifference, neglect, which is not similar to the above).

Valuation standards, curiously, deal with entirely different topics: how much past investments are worth (asset-based methods), how they compare with similar firms today (market-based approach), and how much the firm will be worth in the future based on its return on investment (income-based approach). The three potential values are not averaged, so no investment conclusion can be drawn. From seemingly opposite directions, fundamental and technical analysis meet only at the level of stock market indicators (multipliers), the only ones that link financial data (profit, assets, EBIT(DA), sales) to the stock market price. Similar to technical analysis (based only on past prices, not on economic performance), but using different mathematical methods, are statistical analysis and modern portfolio theory.

Analyses relying only on past prices are based on Famma-type information efficiency theory: the price summarizes all the information about the security, but the price is the result of interaction between a very wide variety of participants with very different knowledge, goals, and interests: from small private individuals to huge investment funds, from scientists with complex methods of analysis to poorly informed dilettantes, from arbitrageurs (who are not interested in the actual quote but only in the spread between two equivalent values) to long-term investors (who do not even look at daily quotes) to speculators who follow subminute intervals. Valuation standards help little in this respect: proof that the share price multiplied by the number of shares is called market capitalization, not to be confused with firm value (which can result, for example, when major M&As are done). And behavioral studies confirm that, in addition to all rational considerations, subjective perceptions, and attitudes, which are very difficult to quantify in monetary terms, play an important role in determining the share price.

No one can guess the exact future. All prospectuses and public offering documents must contain a statement equivalent to "Past performance is no guarantee of future results". But any analysis can only be made on past performance, possibly followed by more or less rational forecasts. And the best forecasts are given by technical analysis because it is the only one that can give recommendations on short, medium, and long-term timeframes. The budget adopted by the OGSM (the basis for financial forecasts) rarely foresees major changes, the statistical analysis does not distinguish between advance-retraction-stationary periods (which have different characteristics in terms of technical analysis), valuation standards do not help much, and behavioral considerations are, in my opinion, at the beginning of the road.

References

Elton, E. J., Gruber, M. J., Brown, S. J., & Goetzmann, W. H. (2014). *Modern portfolio theory and investment analysis*. John Wiley & Sons.

Fabozzi, F. J., & Pachamanova, D. A. (2016). *Portfolio construction and analytics*. Wiley.

Graham, B. (1949). *The intelligent investor. A book of practical council*. Harper & Brothers.

International Valuation Standards Council. *International Valuation Standards. Effective 31 January 2022*. Typeset and printed by Page Bros, Norwich.
Kroese, D. P., & Chan, J. C. C. (2014). *Statistical modeling and computation*. Springer Cham.

CHAPTER 3

Correlations Between Securities and Markets

Abstract "Do not put all the eggs in one basket" is the prudential principle of reducing non-systemic risks. But how should a rational portfolio be built? How do we choose from thousands of companies the least risky and potentially profitable? Theorists use VaR (Value at Risk)—is it representative, as long as the distribution of daily results is not Gaussian? Is intermarket analysis (Murphy) an alternative solution? We will look for the answer to these questions, exploring various theories and practical results. It seems highly important for us if we establish that two titles vary similarly. Unlike modern portfolio theory (which does not distinguish between 2 perfectly correlated securities), we believe that including both in the portfolio reduces non-systemic (specific) risks and, more importantly, allows tracking one and investing in the other, if developments are delayed. Other investment options: futures, vanilla and exotic options, certificates, combined strategies, and arbitrage. How technical analysis helps a complex investment approach.

Keywords Non-systemic risks · Intermarket analysis · Modern portfolio theory · Investment options · Securities

F. C. Dumiter and F. M. Turcaş, *Technical Analysis Applications*,
https://doi.org/10.1007/978-3-031-27416-9_3

3.1 Linkages Between Technical Analysis and Modern Portfolio Theory

The chapter links technical analysis to modern portfolio theory. The role of this chapter is to guide the reader to explore other areas related to financial markets and to show that technical analysis can itself contribute to these theories, perhaps even better than complex mathematical approaches. Because stock markets do not evolve in an exact, perfectly rational, and objective way, technical analysis captures these subjective (sometimes even irrational) aspects better than the far too exact formulaic approaches.

We will also introduce a number of terms related to derivatives: futures, call and put options. What are they? They are bets on the future performance of shares (which constitute the so-called underlying asset). They are widespread and have the advantage that they require a much smaller investment than is needed for a stock portfolio, but the risks are proportionately higher.

Futures are bets on the future performance of the underlying shares: long bets on a rise, and short bets on a fall. It is a zero-sum game: what one loses, the other wins. In reality, a clearing house comes between the speculators who are betting to secure the trades. The advantage is obvious: regardless of the value of the shares, participants in the futures market only put up a margin, a guarantee that they will be able to pay the difference in value if the market moves against their position. Although they have a maturity date, futures contracts can be closed at any time during their life, with the speculator only receiving/paying the difference in price.

Options are, as their name suggests, contracts where the buyer has the option but not the obligation to execute them: call-for-buy contracts and put-for-sell contracts. If it suits, the buyer will execute the contracts and collect the difference between the current value and the contract value; if not, it will let the contract expire, losing only the premium paid on the purchase.

3.2 Correlation—definition and Its Role in Portfolio Theories

The correlation between stocks is one of the most important observations on stock market developments. Strongly positively correlated stocks vary almost similarly, meaning that only one defining asset should be followed, with the others trailing in its wake. If there is also a temporary gap between these positively correlated assets, the advantage becomes even clearer: what happened to the first one is bound to happen to the others.

The best example is the same stock listed on two exchanges. Obviously, the evolution is similar, but gaps can occur and be exploited by investors. The example in Fig. 3.1 is a comparison of the performance of Eli Lilly and Company on the NYSE and Frankfurt XETRA. It can be seen that, although they vary similarly, the correlation is not mathematically exact, and investors can profit from this difference by buying the stock in Germany and selling it in the US.

In our opinion, a portfolio should not hold uncorrelated securities, it should be focused on industries that are growing with stop loss in case the assumption is invalidated. Obviously, this conclusion is only valid for flexible portfolios, big banks, or investment funds cannot switch quickly between industries.

In Fig. 3.2, we see that Eli Lilly and Company is weakly correlated with Oracle and inversely correlated with Tesla.

Arbitrage (hedging) is buying and selling similar assets simultaneously in different markets, taking advantage of price differences at one point in time, knowing that at some future point the two prices will move closer together or even be equal.

The No Arbitrage Principle, recognized in the phrase: "There is no such thing as a free lunch", is a fundamental economic principle in any

Fig. 3.1 LLY listed on 2 stock exchanges (*Source* investing.com)

Fig. 3.2 Uncorrelated and inversely correlated stocks (*Source* investing.com)

free market. It states that you cannot earn more from arbitrage than you would by buying safe bonds in that market. The explanation is simple: if such an opportunity arises, everyone will want to take advantage of it, so the forces governing the market will quickly close the gap.

In the external stock market, there are even automated trading systems that track and exploit arbitrage that occurs at the moment. These occur when the same security is traded on different markets, or between futures and spot prices, when markets do not react quickly enough to sudden price changes. Systems need to be automated because the emergence of arbitrage opportunities is difficult to spot and is quickly absorbed by the market.

Note that the martingale strategy does not belong to the arbitrage category.

Knowing this, the question arises as to how it was possible that during the boom period of the Romanian stock market (the run-up to the "hard landing" of 2008) there were consistent arbitrage opportunities. And not for short periods, but over two whole years. In addition, we will even expose (describe) a logical justification for why many qualified investors did not resort to arbitrage, and well they did.

Arbitrage is the simultaneous buying and selling, in two different markets of one and the same security (or a derivative, directly related to the underlying). The difference between the prices represents the profit made from arbitrage, which is theoretically risk-free: it is certain, regardless of market movements, and can be anticipated numerically at the time the arbitrage is initiated. As long as this relative profit is low or non-existent, arbitrage is not profitable and will not be used by investors except in the case of hedging, which is an insurance of the position held and is intended to reduce the risk of market movements.

According to (Arratia, 2014), if we consider a compound continuous interest bond r, its price P_t at time t will be uniquely determinable as a function of the initial price P_0, as follows:

$$P_t = P_0 * e^{rt} \tag{3.1}$$

If r is constant over the entire period, investing in a bond is risk-free, because we can always determine what its value is.

If a higher return is sought, it is natural to turn to riskier assets such as equities or futures. Again, it is natural that these do not offer the regular possibility of a higher arbitrage gain than non-risky bonds.

It should be noted that investing in financial instruments (as per IFRS 7 Financial Instruments: Disclosures) does involve a number of risks—in addition to market risk—including credit risk, currency risk, interest rate risk, liquidity risk, etc.

We will call **arbitrage opportunities** the situation where there are trading strategies using available instruments in such a way as to generate profit without the risk of loss. One might think that such situations do not exist in reality, but the truth is that these situations occur all the time in stock markets. Everybody who sees the possibility of a risk-free gain tries to take advantage of their existence, and one consequence of their action is that prices change and arbitrage disappears. One conclusion of this is a fundamental observation in the valuation of financial instruments: in the absence of arbitrage, two portfolios with the same value at maturity must have the same price at inception.

A review of the literature in the field sets the state of knowledge.

Moosa (2003) demonstrates that the no-arbitrage principle implies that the difference between the bid and ask rates of a currency in two markets can cover the costs of the transaction (taxes, brokerage fees, and bid-ask spread).

Reverre (2001) presents most of the theoretical and practical aspects of the opportunities offered by arbitrage in financial markets. He also highlights some of the risks of arbitrage, risks confirmed in our example of Romanian market manipulation.

Delbaen and Schachermayer (2006) show that the no-arbitrage principle underlies the entire mathematical apparatus of modern finance, underpinning the valuation of stocks and options.

Javaheri (2005) deals with the subject of arbitrage in the context of volatility issues.

Dubil (2011) illustrates the principle of arbitrage by analyzing: (i) most financial instruments (spot, futures, options, swaps); (ii) financial engineering based on arbitrage between these markets; and (iii) the strategies of each major category of players (banks, funds, individuals).

A book dedicated to individual investors who prefer hedging to naked positions is Whistler (2004).

Fernholtz (2015) shows that there is the possibility of relative arbitrage (between security and the market) in certain market patterns and over certain short time frames.

Farinelli (2015) treats the arbitrage problem from the point of view of Geometric Arbitrage Theory, demonstrating situations where the "*no-free-lunch-with-vanishing-risk condition*" is valid.

Tehranchi (2015) develops arbitrage theory without the assumption of the existence of a numéraire asset (an asset whose price is determined on the basis of another tradable asset).

Aïd, Campi and Lautier (2015) propose an alternative approach to the convergence, at maturity, between the spot price and forward contracts for commodities.

Bid-ask spread was analyzed by Rola (2014) from an arbitrage perspective, with the Cox-Ross-Rubinstein model presented as an application of the study results.

Göncü (2014) demonstrates the existence of arbitrage opportunities in the Black–Scholes model. He considers statistical arbitrage, which has zero initial cost but has the possibility of losing money.

Paul and Wong (2013) analyze in their paper the performance of a portfolio relative to a benchmark market index and show that the relative performance depends on three components, one in terms of energy and two with entropy value.

Franke et al. (2015) demonstrate that one can construct the entire financial theory from the no-arbitrage principle.

The analysis of arbitrage opportunities was carried out for the 2006–2008 period, when the Romanian stock markets operated at satisfactory liquidity parameters, including foreign investors' funds. These are:

- Bucharest Stock Exchange, BVB, which gave the spot price of the shares;
- Sibiu Financial and Commodities Exchange, SIBEX, on which financial derivatives on shares were liquid.

Since corporate bonds were not listed, municipal bonds were illiquid, and government securities were traded mostly on the interbank market and less on the stock market, for the comparison of returns we considered passive bank deposits instead of bonds.

We looked at the most traded derivatives, DESIF5, which is the Sibex futures for the BVB ticker SIF5, an atypical investment fund with good results. For diversification, we also turned to the similarly performing SIF2 ticker. We did not consider another liquid security, Banca Transilvania (TLV), due to frequent share issues, which required artificial price corrections.

Figure 3.3 shows the evolution chart of DESIF5 futures with maturity in December 2007 compared to the SIF5 spot price.

Arbitrage possibilities are evident where the spread (distance between the two charts) is large. But in practice, because markets are not perfect, the question arises as to how large the spread needs to be to benefit from arbitrage.

As this is a boom time for the stock market, it is natural for investors to expect large increases in securities, which is reflected in the futures quotation being much higher than the market price (at least for longer maturities).

The arbitrage is obvious: sell the more expensive asset (short futures position) and buy the cheaper asset (long spot) at the same time. At maturity, the two prices will be equal (the futures position is closed at the spot price), so the final value of the portfolio is known from the outset (no market risk). As they are different exchanges, both will ask for a margin proportional to the value of the investment, i.e. the spot price. We don't have a zero initial investment, but we do have a guaranteed final gain.

The explanation is given by the graph in Fig. 3.4. Investors' expectations of the market's growth rate were extremely high so resorting to

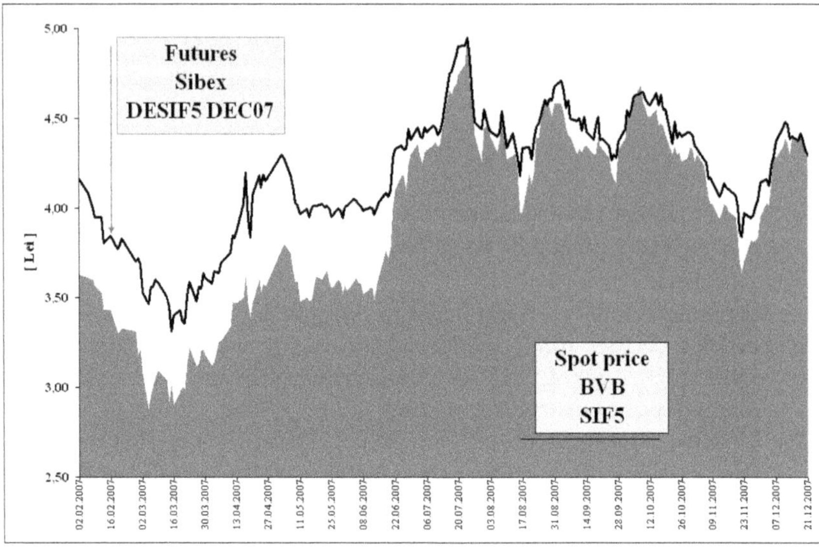

Fig. 3.3 Arbitrage possibilities on DESIF5 DEC07 (*Source* Chart compiled in Excel)

arbitrage would only reduce the potential gains. And the period of stock market exuberance only canceled out any caution, with investors unhappy with small, safe gains. This assertion should also have been valid in mature markets, even though they have experienced previous crises and should have known to be wary.

Figure 3.4 confirms investors' long-term optimism. Until the summer of 2007, investors did the right thing by betting on rising prices at the expense of arbitrage. The line graphs represent futures at different maturities (as expiration approaches, it is natural that the spread will narrow below the arbitrage break-even point and the opportunity will be taken by the start of a new maturity).

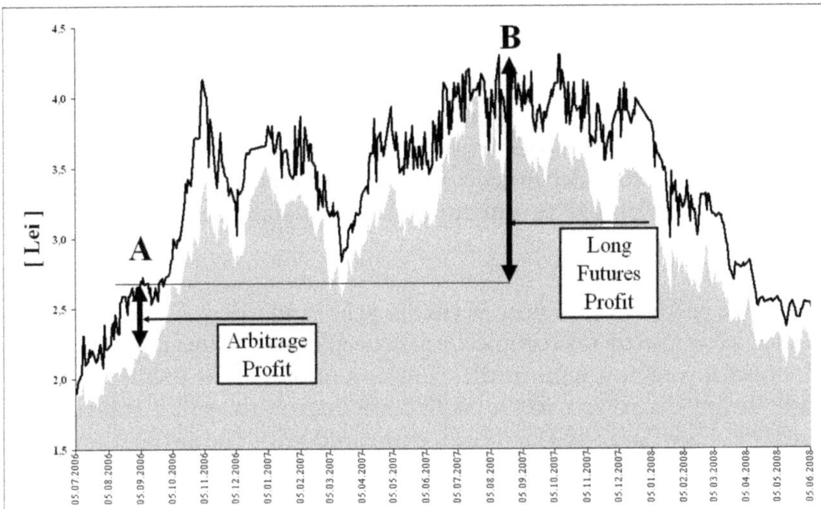

Fig. 3.4 Futures yield vs. arbitrage yield (*Source* Graph generated in Excel and processed in PowerPoint)

3.3 Mathematical Correlation and Practical Correlation (Graphics)

The mathematical correlation used in portfolio theory is a linear relationship between securities, defined by the formula:

$$\text{Correl}(A, B) = \frac{\sum (a - \overline{a})(b - \overline{b})}{\sqrt{\sum (a - \overline{a})^2 (b - \overline{b})^2}} \tag{3.2}$$

where $\overline{a}$ is the mean of vector A, with elements a.

The mathematical correlation has a value $[-1; +1]$, where -1 means exactly inverse variation, 0 means independently varying securities, and $+1$ means perfectly correlated securities.

Mathematical correlation raises some practical problems:

- The number of items in the A and B matrices must be equal, i.e. the securities must be traded on exactly the same days. Although usually not a problem, each security can be stopped from trading on certain days (OGSM, important announcements, capital changes, etc.).

- Correl only checks the linear relationship between securities. For example, Asian stocks should be correlated one day later than US stocks, because the Asian market opens after the US market closes.
- Even non-linear dependence cannot be determined by Correl. Nor is variation similar in direction but with different values correctly captured.

Let's look at the correlation between SIF1 and BRD from a practical point of view, based on technical analysis. We will define the correlation as follows: if we know a priori the evolution of one of the securities (called "base" below), can we make a profit by acting on the other (called "correlated")? How large is this profit compared with the profit that could be made if the change in the correlated security were known directly in advance?

From a practical point of view, it is obvious that this correlation is sufficient to build portfolios protected from non-systemic risks. The investor can track and analyze a single security and act identically on the others, knowing that they behave similarly in relation to market developments (Fig. 3.5).

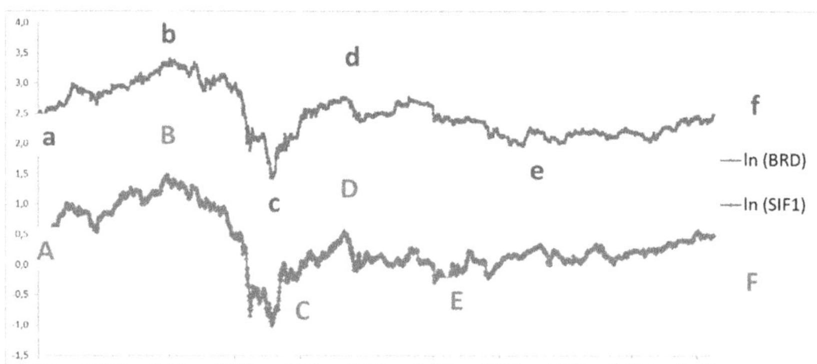

Fig. 3.5 Comparative performance of SIF1 and BRD (*Source* Data taken from bvb.ro and processed in Excel)

The above reasoning is thus applied based on the model presented according to Turcaş et al. (2017):

- We set the points of interest on the chart of the underlying issuer, SIF1 in our case. These are: initial point **A**, absolute maximum **B**, absolute minimum **C**, relative maximum **D**, relative minimum **E**, and final point **F**. These data are assumed to be known by investors to initiate long/short positions.
- Correspondingly, on the same dates, investors consider taking the same positions on BRD. If there is a long signal on SIF1, take a long position on BRD, if the signal on the underlying security is short, take a short position on the correlated one.
- For the correlated security, the return on investment is calculated as follows, based on the correlation strategy.
- For comparison, similar points are defined on the BRD's back chart, noted similarly but in lowercase. A good synchronization can already be observed, with points **b**, **c**, and **d** being extremely close to their counterparts on the underlying security.
- The return on investment in BRD is calculated without taking into account the correlation strategy, called direct return.

The returns of the two investments can now be compared in order to conclude the effectiveness of the strategy based on the correlation of securities. The result of 84% is satisfactory for any investor: the two securities prove to be practically correlated, a common portfolio being partly protected from risks specific to individual issuers.

We make the important observation that the above reasoning is different from the traditional interpretation of the CORREL statistical function. If we had considered the above strategy on a daily basis (when the underlying stock rose we take a long position on the correlated stock; similarly, when it fell – > short) the return would have been only 53%.

The problem now is to determine calculation algorithms that will automate to the greatest extent possible the process shown in Table 3.1.

3.4 Principles of Portfolio Construction

In modern portfolio theory, the focus is on looking for uncorrelated stocks so that the portfolio is as protected as possible from market falls. But this principle is of little value to small investors, who are looking for gains and not necessarily safe in the stock market. For them, it would be

Table 3.1 Comparison of direct investment returns with that resulting from correlation

Date	*SIF1*	*BRD*			*Position*	*Correl. Profit BRD*	*Direct Profit BRD*
02.08.05	1,6100	11,4000	**A**	a	Buy		
24.07.07	4,3800	28,0000	**B**		Short	16,60	
08.08.07		29,7000		b			18,30
24.02.09	0,3650	3,7300	**C**	c	Long	24,27	25,97
01.04.10		15,9000		d	Short		12,17
02.04.10	1,7300	15,9000	**D**			12,17	
07.12.11	0,8400	11,0000	**E**		Long	4,90	
07.12.12		7,1250		e			8,78
06.11.15	1,6160	11,9600	**F**	f	Sell of	0,96	4,84
					TOTAL	**58,90**	**70,05**
						84%	

Source Own processing

preferable to get out of falling markets and into rising ones. This is the theory of Intermarket variations, which is based on the fact that money has to flow and the economy cannot stand still.

An idea of how to take advantage of market fluctuations is given in an example from the Romanian market.

The following example starts from the assumption that we are predicting a market movement and want to act accordingly. Here, of course, art will consist in accurately determining forecasts, but broadly speaking, technical analysis gives us enough elements for extensive movements. The example was actually carried out on the market during that period (Fig. 3.6).

The graphs are drawn in Mathcad, a program in which the calculations were also made.

At the beginning of the period, we foresee the following for the evolution of the SIF5 title:

- From 2.26 (July, 2006) the quotation will tend to 4.00, which will probably be reached in January 2007.
- In March 2007, as every year, the quotation will decrease, to a value that will be higher than the initial quotation.

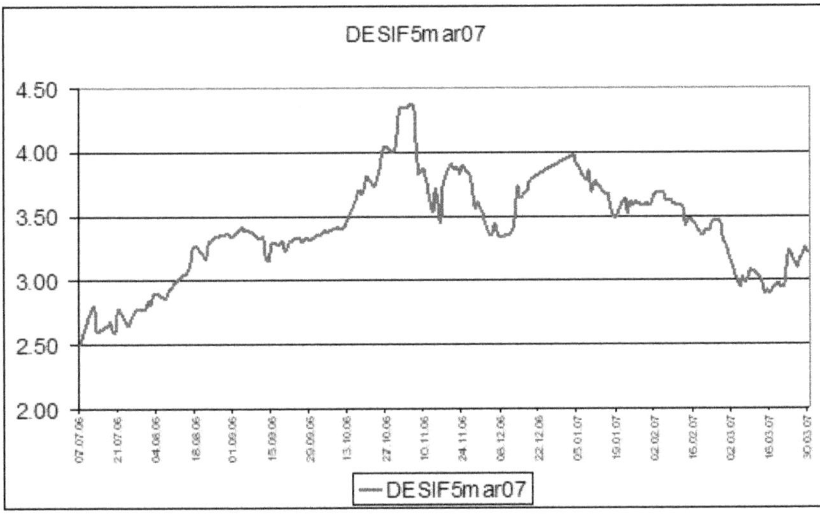

Fig. 3.6 Estimated evolution of SIF5 (*Source* Own processing in Mathcad)

These are our initial predictions and are quite simple and logical.

The first option would be to purchase long-call contracts, at exercise prices as low as possible (but obviously higher than the initial quotation of 2.50 for DESIF5mar07) and with the lowest possible premiums (premiums are irrevocably paid at the time of purchase of the contract). Of course, we will not be able to meet both conditions. Let's say we purchased long-call contracts in 3.50, with a premium of 0.10. This means that we paid 100 lei for each contract (the premium of 0.10 × the multiplier of 1,000), this being our only cost and risk (the transaction cost, of 1.5 lei/contract, is absolutely negligible). If the futures quote exceeds 3.50, the options contract goes into the money, and if it exceeds 3.60 lei (the exercise price is 3.50 + the first 0.10), the option enters the profit (Figs. 3.7 and 3.8).

Starting with 16.10.06, the forecast is made and the counter options enter the profit. On 02.11.07, the futures quotation DESIF5mar07 is 4.35. We already consider that this is exaggerated (with 0.77 lei/action over the spot!), the technical analysis gives us signals of return of trend, and our gain is already substantial ([4.35–3.60] × 1,000 = 750 lei/contract). Around this point (or when the market is already starting

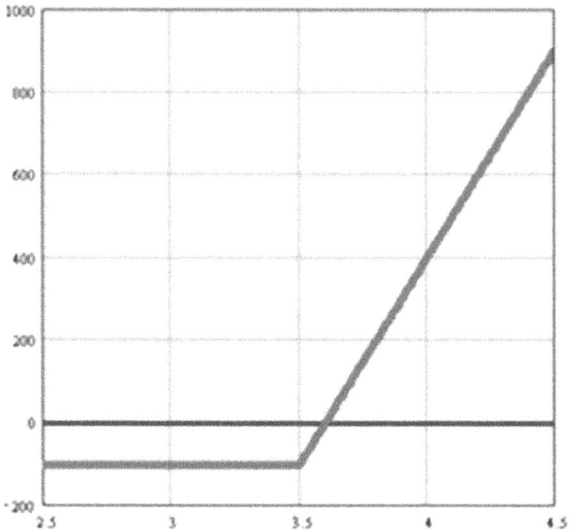

Fig. 3.7 First investment: call option (*Source* Own processing in Mathcad)

to fall), the call contract is redeemed by selling a futures contract. The option should not be exercised: whenever it is available to us, we are not taking the margin for the futures contract (the contract is "covered") and BMFMS will calculate this profit as available to us anyway. The only risk is the loss of the potential profit if the quote had further increased. Thus, we made a synthetic long put that is directly in the money. Again it turns out that we have reasoned correctly and there is a significant decrease in the quotation. At the moment, our gain remains the same, but we are waiting for the end of the drop. We do not consider that we could also guess the small price variations, but in December we begin to suspect that it has already dropped too much (3.33 on 08.12.06) and we expect it to increase again, especially in January 2007. Obviously, we close the short on futures (through a long purchase) and check our portfolio: we won 920 lei/contract ([short at 4.35—long in 3.33—first call 0.10] x multiplier 1,000) and we still own the horses in 3.50! (Fig. 3.9).

After the increase in January 2007, we repeat the realization of a synthetic well, purchasing short futures (say, at 3.92 on 04.01.07). Again, the market falls, and our forecast is confirmed, but this time, we assume

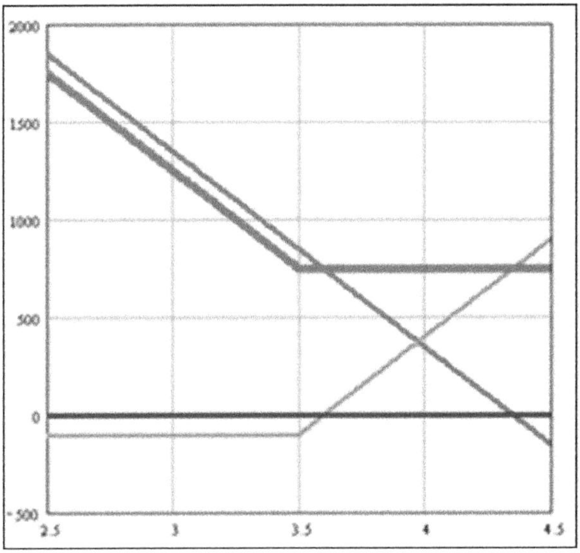

Fig. 3.8 The synthetic stink is made of a long call and short futures (*Source* Own processing in Mathcad)

that we no longer know how to estimate the price target per withdrawal. Under these conditions, we can sell the covered well (we assume the strike price is 3.00, with the premium of 0.10), thus blocking the potential gain (if the quote falls below 3.00–0.10 = 2.90) but ensuring the gain of the premium. We made a fence, its profit being between [3.92–3.50] × 1,000 = 420 lei/contract if the quotation at maturity is over 3.50 and [3.92–3.00] × 1,000 = 920 lei/contract if the quotation is below 3.00 (Fig. 3.10).

The premium originally paid for the call contract was offset by the premium received on the put contract. It is noticed the non-exercise of the call contract will be exercised automatically at the due date (if this is still the case). Globally, by investing 100 lei/ contract, we achieved a gross profit, without tax (16%, being held for a term below 1 year) and without the transaction costs (which in total would be 15 lei), between 1,440 lei and 1,920 lei. And that is without using a special accuracy of forecasts! The only difficulty is the low liquidity of the options market.

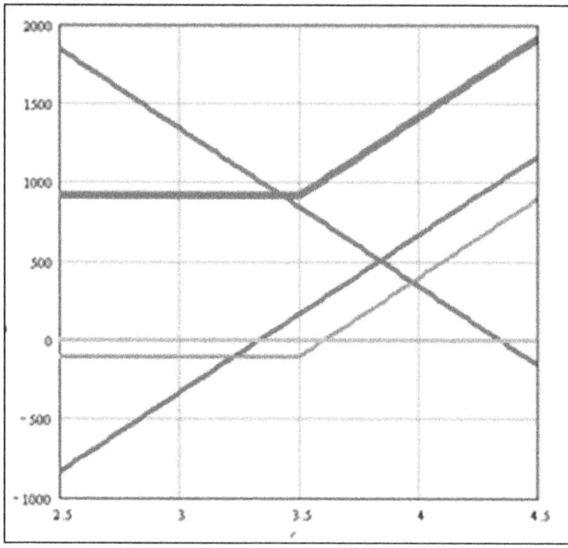

Fig. 3.9 Chart of the remaining call, which also includes the gain obtained (*Source* Own processing in Mathcad)

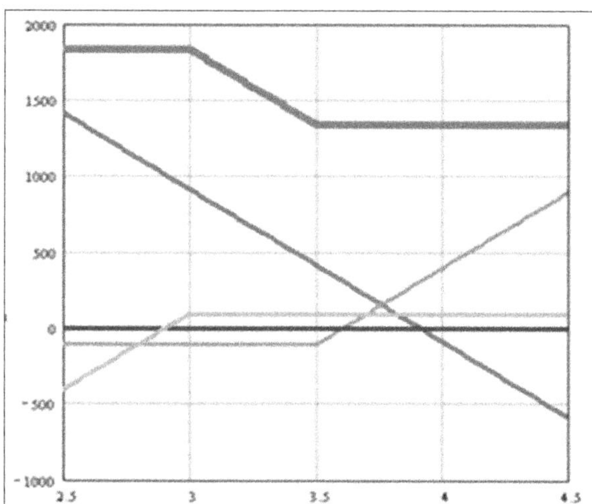

Fig. 3.10 Fence (*Source* Own processing in Mathcad)

Let's take another example. Gold is a defensive asset: it doesn't lose value but it can't grow spectacularly either, as world production and consumption are relatively stable and predictable. When the stock market falls, it is natural for gold to rise, because investors tend to stop speculating and move into safer assets. Conversely, the stock market rises much faster in times of boom than gold, so investors will satisfy their need for adrenaline (Fig. 3.11).

And in some periods, the dollar's movement is inverse to the stock market, as shown in Fig. 3.12.

Murphy shows in his paper a whole theory of cyclical market variations and their alternation. We don't present them here because, in our opinion, these variations and cyclicality are only temporary: in the long run, market growth is very well approximated logarithmically (Fig. 3.13).

We'll stay in the realm of stock markets and look at the correlation of stocks with the overall market index.

The best indicator of the linear change of stocks relative to the market is β.

In valuation theory, the APT (Arbitrage Pricing Theory) method of the market approach involves using the correlation between the valued security and the industry:

$$R = R_f + \beta\left(R_b - R_f\right) \tag{3.3}$$

Fig. 3.11 Gold vs. shares (*Source* investing.com)

Fig. 3.12 The inverse relationship between the dollar and the stock market (*Source* investing.com)

Fig. 3.13 Intermarket charts (*Source* investing.com)

where R is the expected return (CAPM in the DCF model), Rf is the risk-free rate (e.g. AAA-rated government or bond yield), Rb is the expected benchmark index return (e.g. the main stock index), and β is the industry-market covariance.

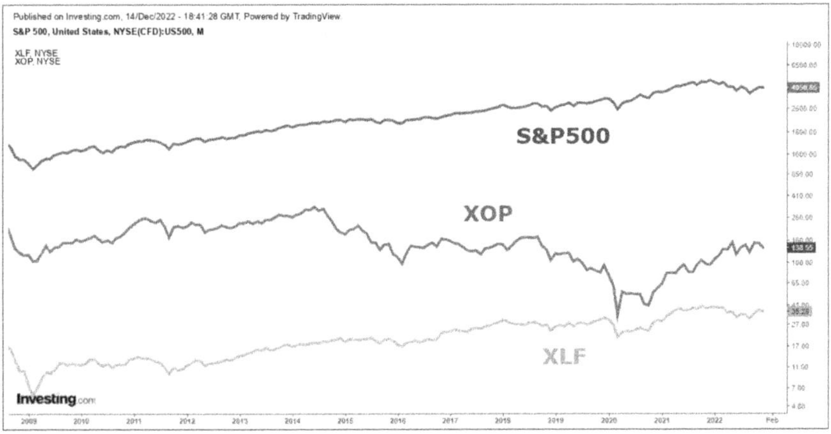

Fig. 3.14 Correlation between EFTs and market index (*Source* investing.com)

Let's look at some practical examples (Fig. 3.14).

Financial Select Sector SPDR® Fund (XLF) has a $\beta = 1.1$ because it varies similarly to the S&P 500 market index.

SPDR® S&P Oil & Gas Exploration & Production ETF (XOP) has a $\beta = 2.54$ because it varies differently than the market.

Because it varies inversely than the market, Akero Therapeutics Inc (AKRO) has a $\beta = -0.9$ (Fig. 3.15).

3.5 Finis Coronat Opus

We draw some conclusions on investment strategies:

- Diversification: Don't put all your eggs in one basket. A key person in the firm may disappear, fraud may occur, market manipulation, and hostile takeover. But in our view, diversification should only target multiple firms in the same field, industry, or category and only in exceptional cases be arbitrage or hedging.
- Let your profits run, and cut your losses short. Don't get out until the uptrend is confirmed broken. There is no point in maintaining a losing position. It is no good going against the wind, so it is no good staying on the losing side of the trend. Setting a take profit price is not mandatory, but a stop loss is.

Fig. 3.15 An example (among few) of negative β (*Source* investing.com)

- Money has to flow. If one market does badly, another is likely to do well. Rarely does money go out of the market altogether. If one stock is doing badly, it is worth looking for the ones that are doing well. However, in stock markets, there are ways to win even if the market goes down (futures, put options, certificates, short sells).

And some tactics that can be winning:

- Act only when there are signals of a trend change: crossing of averages, violation of trend lines, signals of patterns, indicators, or oscillators.
- If the market is trending up, buy stocks with the highest β, because that means they will perform in the direction of the market, but much more aggressively.
- We do not recommend stocks with low β (negative β are very few, irrelevant). They should be watched independently, they are in their own world. If the market goes down, you better hedge if you don't want to exit the market altogether.
- With regularity, there is no way to buy at the bottom and sell at the top. When momentum picks up, markets have plenty of room to rise on the uptrend. It is perfect if we buy on the rise and sell as soon as the trend weakens.

References

Aïd, R., Campi, L., & Lautier, D. (2015). A note on the spot-futures no-arbitrage relations in a trading-production model for commodities. *arXiv:1501.00273v2 [q-fin.MF] 27 April 2015.*

Arratia, A. (2014). *Computational finance.* Atlantis Press.

Delbaen, F., & Schachermayer, W. (2006). *The mathematics of arbitrage.* Springer-Verlag.

Dubil, R. (2011). *Financial engineering and arbitrage in the financial markets.* John Wiley & Sons, Ltd.

Farinelli, S. (2015). Geometric arbitrage and spectral theory. *arXiv:1509.03264v1 [q-fin.MF] 2 September 2015.*

Fernholtz, R. (2015). An example of short-term relative arbitrage. *arXiv:1510.02292v1 [q-fin.MF] 8 October 2015.*

Franke, J., Härdle, W. K., & Hafner, C. M. (2015). *Statistics of financial markets.* Springer, Universitext.

Göncü, A. (2014). Statistical arbitrage in the Black-Scholes Framework. *arXiv:1406.5646v4 [q-fin.MF] 30 August 2014.*

Javaheri, A. (2005). *Inside volatility arbitrage: The secrets of skewness.* John Wiley & Sons, Inc.

Moosa, I. A. (2003). *International financial operations arbitrage, hedging, speculation, financing, and investment.* Palgrave Macmillan.

Paul, S., & Wong, T.-K. L. (2013). Energy, entropy, and arbitrage. *arXiv:1308.5376v1 [q-fin.PM] 25 August 2013.*

Reverre, S. (2001). *The complete arbitrage deskbook.* McGraw-Hill.

Rola, P. (2014). Arbitrage in markets with bid-ask spreads the fundamental theorem of asset pricing in finite discrete time markets with bid-ask spreads and a money account. *arXiv:1407.3372v1 [q-fin.PR] 12 July 2014.*

Tehranchi, M. R. (2015). Arbitrage theory without a numeraire. *arXiv:1410.2976v2 [q-fin.MF] 4 July 2015.*

Turcaş, F., Brezeanu, P., Dumiter, F., Fărcaş, P., & Coroiu, S. I. (2017). Using technical analysis for portfolio selection and post-investment analysis. *Economic Research – Ekonomska Istraživanja, 30*(1), 14–30.

Whistler, M. (2004). *Trading pairs: Capturing profits and hedging risk with statistical arbitrage strategies.* John Wiley & Sons, Inc.

CHAPTER 4

Charts Used in Technical Analysis

Abstract In this chapter, we dive into the essence of technical analysis: a brief overview of chart types and their usefulness; automated trading systems; relevant chart points to automate their interpretation; and the order of charts in technical analysis. It seems simple to look at a chart. But we will also interpret splits, capital increases, the influence of dividends and news. We'll show why comparative charts can be misleading, explain false confirmations, and understand divergences between indicators. Look at the following image (finviz.com). It graphically shows the evolution of the main blue chips in the US market. You can immediately see how they have evolved and decide which ones you are interested in. All the data can easily be entered into a computer, but how will it be able to discern which stock is more interesting? In fact, the question is: "What are we making him look at?" "What do we find really interesting about a chart?"

Keywords Non-systemic risks · Intermarket analysis · Modern portfolio theory · Investment options · Securities

The complex phenomenon of stock markets starts from the evolution of the financial ecosystem was analyzed by Strumeyer and Swammy (2017) by presenting some important actual challenges in finance, *lato sens*,

F. C. Dumiter and F. M. Turcaş, *Technical Analysis Applications*,
https://doi.org/10.1007/978-3-031-27416-9_4

and in capital markets, *stricto sensu*; these challenges tackle the worldwide evolution of the capital market, the several underlying risks, risk management, and the challenges ahead. Schabacker (2020) developed an interesting guide for investors with a special focus on technical analysis by revealing several aspects such as trends, resistance areas, formations, and patterns. In the aftermath, Amin (2021) analyzed the capital market through the decision-making behavior of an investor by taking into account the connections between stock market development and ethnic respectively religious diversity.

Kuznetsov (2006) developed a practical guide for the quantitative professional which act on the stock market by revealing some of the Wall Street business models with a special focus oriented on the trading techniques applied to the financial markets. The linkages between stock markets and foreign exchange markets were analyzed by Gavrilov (2015), especially with regard to the connections manifested between returns obtained by the forex markets with those of the stock market. Brandimarte (2018) makes a comprehensive analysis of the financial markets by gathering important aspects such as financial management, mathematics, and statistics, techniques oriented toward innovative finance and risk management.

The securities aspect was an important aspect debated in the economic literature. Simmons (2002) developed a study for financial analysts regarding managing the operational risk with a special focus on securities transactions and their settlements aspects. Suangtho (2012) provides an empirical analysis of the connections between the UK stock traded and other emerging and developing market stock exchanges. Other specialists such as Schwartz et al. (2017) developed studies that focus on regulatory changes in securities, the evolution of market quality, and the structural changes which are still needed in the stock market. Finally, Singh and Yadav (2021) developed a complex handbook tackling the actual aspects of portfolio management and security analysis with a special enactment upon returns, price, and risk multiplies.

In this chapter, we have made the charts on these public sites. In no way is this hidden advertising, we simply use these programs.

The charts can be found on thousands of sites; all they do is put the data received from the exchanges on a chart. The problem is interpreting them—that's where the analyst comes in.

Every broker and every venue has free charting facilities; it is not necessary for the investor to buy a specialized program until much later stages.

4.1 Types of Charts

Most charts plot the evolution of the stock market price over time. In this study, it will be seen that there are also charts with dots and figures that do not depend on time but only reflect the evolution of prices, but these are less used.

The first classification of charts is according to the scale on which the prices are plotted: linear or logarithmic.

The normal scale is the most common—most technical analysis procedures are applied to this type of chart.

It should be noted that no single chart represents all trades, all price movements. In mature markets, trades are calculated in milliseconds—there are even High-Frequency Trading (HFT) procedures with the help of modern computers. Users cannot process this amount of data nor do they need to know all the trades. Thus, the idea of freeing up charts and simplifying them was born.

Thus, the simplest charts take into account only the closing values at the end of the day. These are called line charts and are delivered to users at time intervals from 1 minute (sometimes even subminute) to hourly, daily, weekly, monthly, yearly.

For example, in Fig. 4.1 it was plotted the minute-by-minute change in Boeing's share price on July 1, 2022. HFT traders, intraday speculators, and some technical analysts will turn to this chart to "draw conclusions and to prepare and implement their strategies". But for most investors, not every small price change is relevant; they are watching the stock's performance over a longer period. They will turn to the daily chart, drawn in Fig. 4.2. Here, the whole of the previous chart boils down to a single point (the highlighted one) and a single value (139.84—the closing price, at the end of the day).

Similarly, the weekly and monthly charts further encapsulate the price evolution curve, presenting investors with a summarized overview.

However, the monthly chart, for example, oversimplifies the price trend. This can sometimes obscure broad market movements as well as some technical analysis signals (e.g. penetration of trend lines). This has led to the use of Japanese candlesticks, which summarize the evolution

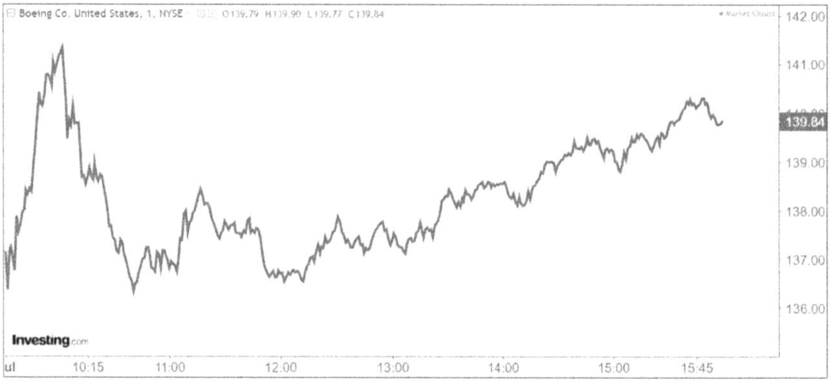

Fig. 4.1 Boeing shares prices on July 1, 2022 (*Source* investing.com)

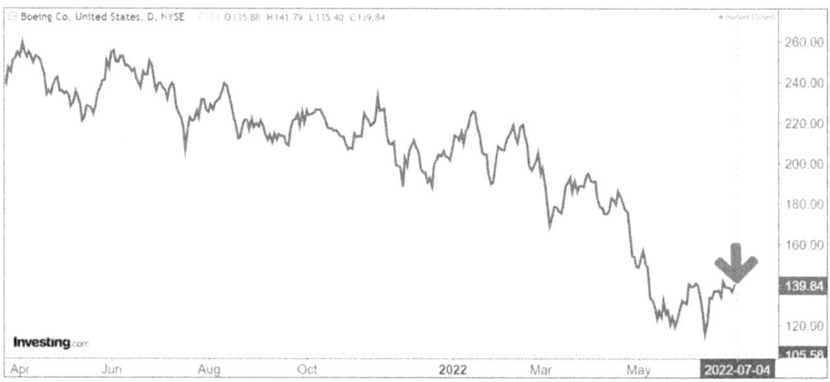

Fig. 4.2 Daily chart (*Source* investing.com)

of a month on the monthly chart—previously a simple dot on the chart, now Fig. 4.3 with the following meaning: the body of the candle is green if it has risen over the period (Open lower than Close) and red otherwise; the shadows reflect the highs and lows.

The bar charts are similar, in which the opening is represented by a small segment on the left, the closing by a segment on the right, the body of the candle being red if it has declined and green if it has risen during the period represented; the length of the body is the distance between the high and the low (Fig. 4.4).

Fig. 4.3 Candlestick chart (*Source* investing.com) (Color figure online)

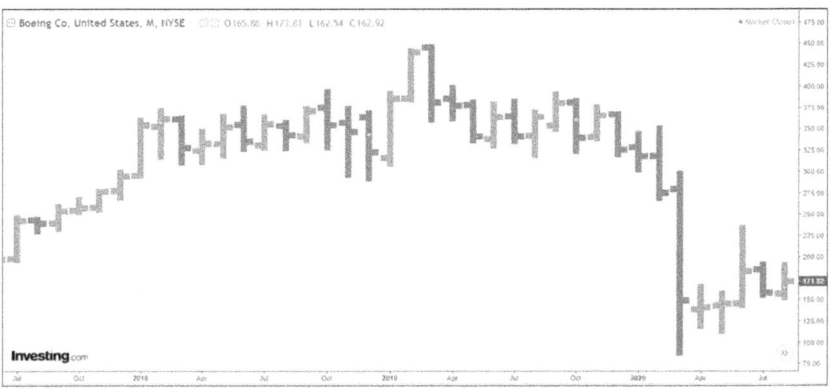

Fig. 4.4 Bars (*Source* investing.com) (Color figure online)

This type of representation gave birth to the Japanese formations technique. These are sequences of candlesticks, with specific names, that are bullish or bearish in character. Figure 4.5 shows an example of such a Japanese formation, automatically detected by the investing.com program and briefly explained. It can be seen that the Bearish character has been confirmed, with the price falling after the completion of the formation.

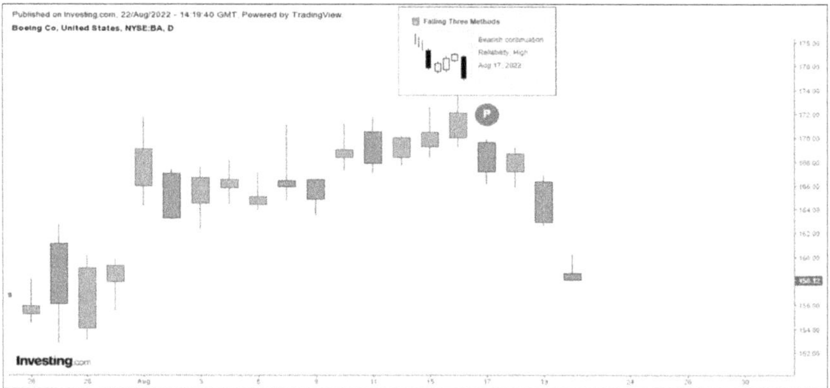

Fig. 4.5 Japanese formations (*Source* investing.com)

4.2 Electronic Interpretation of Data

For example, when trend lines are drawn automatically, situations arise where they have no meaning on the chart: lows in descending charts or highs in ascending charts joined by lines, absolutely minor trend lines plotted on charts (Fig. 4.6).

Computer analysis of data is the basis for automated predictions, which can sometimes be inconsistent. Figure 4.7 shows the screen with the recommendations based on the computerized technical analysis of the issuer Teraplast SA, listed on BSE.

It is worth noting that the recommendations seem contradictory: strong sell vs. strong buy on different timeframes—daily and weekly. In detail, it can also notice how exactly these forecasts were generated (Fig. 4.8), exemplifying SNP OMV Petrom SA, the main company focused on the extraction and processing of hydrocarbons and natural gas in Romania. The explanation of why a good stock (see longer-term recommendations) appears undesirable in the short term is the recent drop noted with the blue arrow in Fig. 4.9. In the longer run, the decline is insignificant and does not influence the parameters of the mathematical calculation implemented in the software. But in the short term, it signals an oversell, possibly stemming from panic. Here, however, the underlying cause of the decline, namely dividend distributions, needs to be analyzed. The shareholder's wealth does not differ much, whether he sells the shares before the ex-date, keeps them despite the drop but collects the dividends.

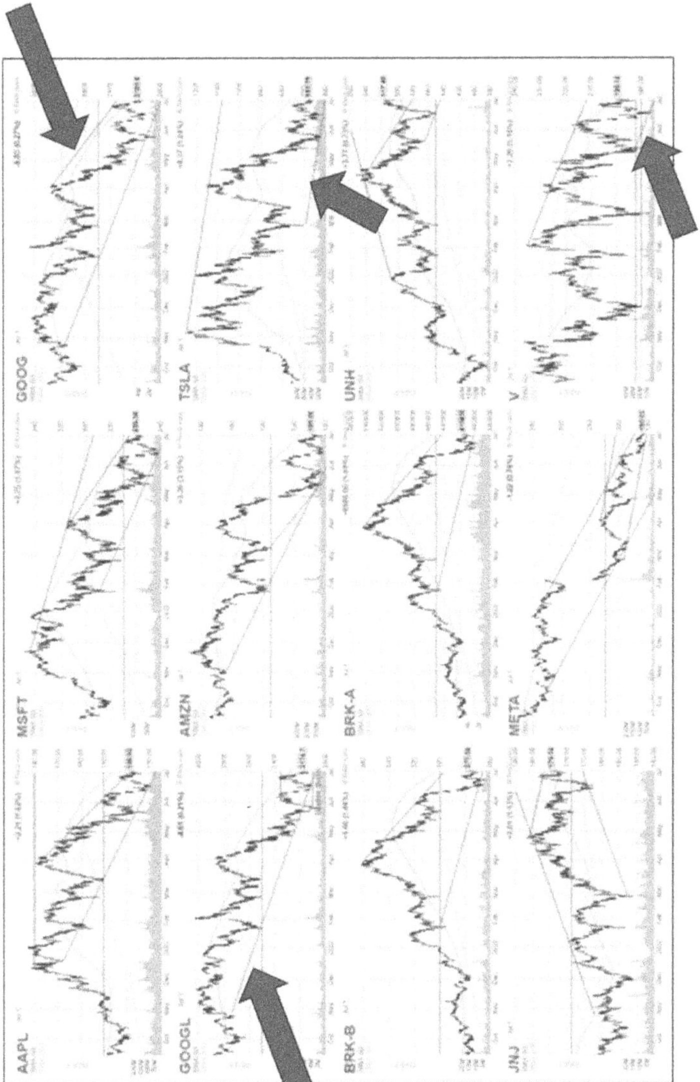

Fig. 4.6 Useless trend lines automatically drawn (*Source* https://finviz.com/screener.ashx?v=211&o=-marketcap)

Technical Summary »

Type	Daily	Weekly	Monthly
Moving Averages	Neutral	Buy	Buy
Technical Indicators	Strong Sell	Strong Buy	Strong Buy
Summary	Sell	Strong Buy	Strong Buy

Fig. 4.7 Investing.com recommendations (*Source* investing.com)

It is a clear example that technical analysis needs to be correlated with fundamental analysis, with news about events in the company and even with macroeconomic realities.

4.3 Automatic Trading Signals

As will be discussed in detail later, financial analysts use a host of indicators and oscillators in an attempt to define the character of the market: bearish or bullish. Each of these has a mathematical expression, which helps to use calculators for impersonal, accurate data analysis. Based on these results, the software can be developed to automatically manage portfolios.

For instance, moving averages are simple (arithmetic) or exponential averages of prices over the last few days. The trading rule is simple: if the average is below the current share price, it is a good time to buy/hold. If the price is below the average of the last periods, it is not good to be or enter the market.

Let's look at an example: it is considered the prices of the American company Boeing (BA) and the moving average over the last 130 periods (weeks, in the example chosen), according to Fig. 4.10. An automated system trading on the basis of the intersection of the 130-week moving average with the weekly stock price would have the following operations and results:

- At point **A**, it would go long (buy) because the average crosses above the price.
- At point **B**, it would close long and go short (sell) because the average goes below the price. The profit so far would be equal to the length of the green arrow (the vertical distance between **B** and **A**).

ROSNP Technical Analysis

Daily Weekly Monthly

Summary: SELL

Moving Averages:	NEUTRAL	Buy (6)	Sell (6)
Technical Indicators:	STRONG SELL	Buy (1)	Sell (7)

Pivot Points » Aug 21, 2022 07:55AM GMT

Name	S3	S2	S1	Pivot Points	R1	R2	R3
Classic	0.4810	0.4825	0.4855	0.4870	0.4900	0.4915	0.4945
Fibonacci	0.4825	0.4842	0.4853	0.4870	0.4887	0.4898	0.4915
Camarilla	0.4873	0.4877	0.4881	0.4870	0.4889	0.4893	0.4897
Woodie's	0.4818	0.4829	0.4863	0.4874	0.4908	0.4919	0.4953
DeMark's	-	-	0.4863	0.4874	0.4908	-	-

Technical Indicators » Aug 21, 2022 07:55AM GMT

Name	Value	Action
RSI(14)	46.505	Neutral
STOCH(9,6)	20.400	Sell
STOCHRSI(14)	5.352	Oversold
MACD(12,26)	0.002	Buy
ADX(14)	58.457	Sell
Williams %R	-88.393	Oversold
CCI(14)	-61.3968	Sell
ATR(14)	0.0094	Less Volatility
Highs/Lows(14)	-0.0124	Sell
Ultimate Oscillator	44.269	Sell
ROC	-8.208	Sell
Bull/Bear Power(13)	-0.0160	Sell

Buy: 1 Sell: 7 Neutral: 1
Summary: STRONG SELL

Moving Averages » Aug 21, 2022 07:55AM GMT

Period	Simple	Exponential
MA5	0.4873 Sell	0.4867 Sell
MA10	0.4910 Sell	0.4927 Sell
MA20	0.5049 Sell	0.4938 Sell
MA50	0.4758 Buy	0.4798 Buy
MA100	0.4525 Buy	0.4635 Buy
MA200	0.4451 Buy	0.4457 Buy

Buy: 6 Sell: 6
Summary: NEUTRAL

Fig. 4.8 Mathematical basis for the recommendation (*Source* investing.com)

Fig. 4.9 SNP daily chart (*Source* investing.com) (Color figure online)

Fig. 4.10 Strategy based on the intersection of the averages with the price chart (*Source* investing.com) (Color figure online)

- The short position would still remain open; the actual gain would be the vertical distance between **B** and **C** (the length of the red arrow). The position would close when the price would exceed the average.

The results are quite satisfactory, but it misses the potential gain between **D** and **E** because the average is too long (the 130-week interval is too broad) to capture the movement (which occurred in one year = 52 weeks). Obviously, the solution is to use shorter averages (which capture the movements more accurately), but that risks generating many more trades (which costs, due to commissions). Figure 4.11 shows that the 50-week average would capitalize on the **DE**'s growth interval, but the disadvantage would be that in the **F** area it would make a lot of unnecessary trades (many intersections of the price with the average, although it remains almost constant → no gains can be recorded). A finer solution would be that the long/short position is taken only if the longer average also crosses above/below the shorter average.

It is noted that the functioning of these automatic signals is highly dependent on the issuer and market developments. Thus, certain indicators are very useful in dynamic markets (trending), but useless in markets that are stagnating (moving laterally). In the above example, no average helps us in the **F**-zone and on the weekly timeframe; either choose another range or use other indicators. For stock market aficionados, we think the most reasonable advice is useless: it was a time when they had better stay out of the market, or look for other stocks.

Fig. 4.11 Advantages and disadvantages of shorter averages (*Source* investing.com)

4.4 Graphical Depiction of Securities and Their Evolution in the Market Using Important Points on the Chart

A note on graphical depiction is how corporate operations (events) are represented.

The first important event is the distribution of dividends, which increases shareholders' wealth. Dividends are distributed to those who own the shares on a certain date, called the record date in Romania. Regardless of when the shares were bought or how long they have been held, it is only important for the payment of dividends that the shares are registered in the investor's portfolio at the end of the record date. As settlement of transactions is not instantaneous but after a certain time ($T + 2$ days on the Bucharest Stock Exchange), the ex-date (the date on which the shares must be held) is $T - 1$, where T is the record date. Whoever buys the shares before the ex-date receives dividends, whoever sells them before the ex-date does not.

Let's look at Fig. 4.12. After a very good 2020, Teraplast SA (TRP), an important producer in the plastics industry at a national level in Romania and at a European level, decides in its OGSM, at the beginning of 2021, to distribute dividends, with ex-date 12.07.2021. Anyone who bought shares the day before receives dividends, even though they did not participate at all (were not a shareholder) in 2020, the year in which the profit from which dividends are distributed was made.

It should also be noted that the dividend yield is quite high (0.13 RON, at a current share price of 0.76 RON), so the chart has a drop, due to the fact that the share recipient is richer than the non-recipient. Technical analysis should keep in mind this downward drop is artificial (not covered by indicators nor oscillators) and that it is usually covered relatively quickly if the market is not in recession.

Share splits and consolidations of nominal value are also important. These involve changing the number of shares and hence their trading value, as the same value of the company is split over a different number of shares.

Let's look at the charts of Banca Transilvania (ticker TLV on the Bucharest Stock Exchange), the most important bank in Romania. It has decided to increase the nominal value (share consolidation) by 10 times, from 1 leu/share to 10 lei/share. Naturally, the number of shares was reduced by 10 times and the share price increased by 10, because the

Fig. 4.12 Effects of dividend distributions (*Source* Chart from investing.com)

wealth of each shareholder does not have to change (the operation did not affect the overall value of the issuer).

If the chart would not be corrected for such transactions, it would look like Fig. 4.13. The chart is correct (prices actually found in the market), but the jumps can be interpreted as either corporate transactions or operational events arising from the firm's activity. Thus, technical analysis software corrects the latter chart to provide the continuity needed to process indicators and chart patterns (Fig. 4.14). This chart adjustment actually ensures the consistency of the graphical representation of shareholder wealth, except for dividend distributions (for this the chart is not adjusted—because on mature exchanges dividends do not usually exceed 3 ÷ 5%, so the adjustments are minor).

Let's also look at the effect of the news on stock prices.

"Coca-Cola lost $4 billion in market value after soccer star Cristiano Ronaldo suggested people drink water instead"[1] is a typical headline after a footballer at a press conference removed the bottles of soda advertised by the sponsor and recommended drinking water. Coca-Cola's chart of the period leading up to the event is shown in Fig. 4.15. Obviously, if we hadn't drawn attention to the period, no one could have detected

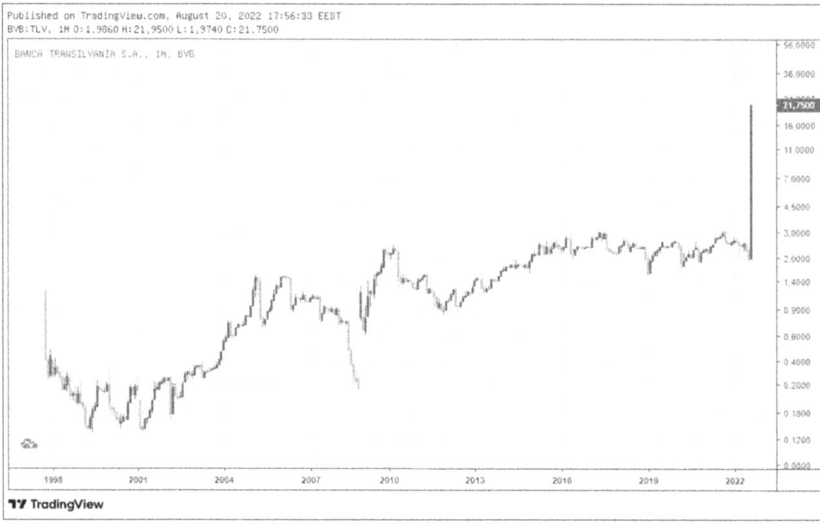

Fig. 4.13 Unadjusted prices for TLV (*Source* Chart from investing.com)

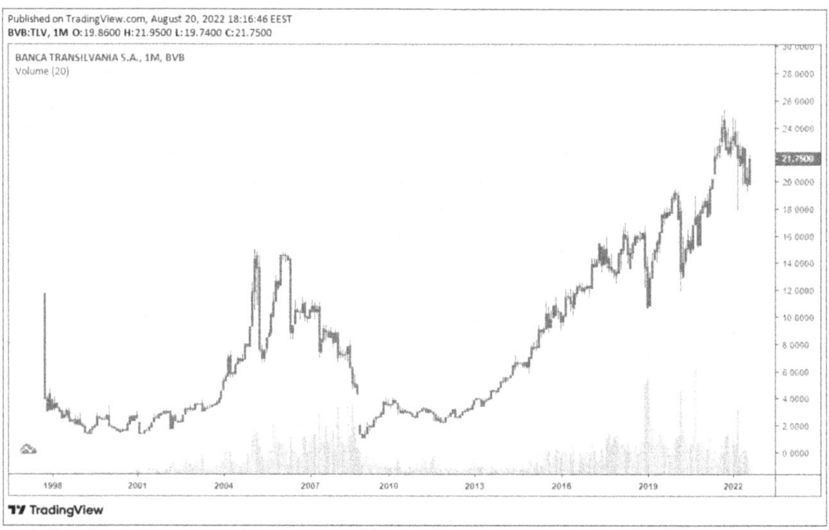

Fig. 4.14 Adjusted prices TLV (*Source* Chart from investing.com)

that drop. It's just an example of news that accentuates an actually non-existent "event".

Technical analysis also teaches us that there are no good or bad stocks; there are only right and wrong moments to enter/exit the market. Let's look at the chart in Fig. 4.16. After the recent energy and microchip crises, it is clear from the chart that stock market investments should have been focused on energy and not technology.

Fig. 4.15 News influence (*Source* Chart from investing.com)

Fig. 4.16 Comparison of current S&P energy and semiconductor indices (*Source* Chart from investing.com)

Let's just note two things. First, leaving the scale intact, let's move the graph backward in time. Surprisingly, for the same investment horizon of a few months, we find that a year and a half ago it was better to stay away from energetics and invest in modern technologies such as semiconductors (Fig. 4.17).

Second, let's go back to Fig. 4.16, but enlarge the chart—equivalent to setting a shorter investment horizon. Figure 4.18 again suggests that if we adopt a speculative (hit and run) investment policy, in the short run we are better off focusing on technology.

However, how is it possible that all these seemingly contradictory results are simultaneously true? Technical analysis confirms that it is possible; moreover, it is quite natural that it should be so. Market fluctuations, inexplicable by fundamental or behavioral analysis, are natural, predictable and relatively easy for technical analysts to exploit. They rely on a simple rule: no stock is bad or good; there are only bad and good strategies.

A convincing example that illustrates the above idea is the chart of General Electric (stock ticker: GE). The famous company was part of the Dow index for more than a century (kicked out in 2018) and currently on a downtrend for more than 22 years. Figure 4.19 shows the 1-month chart of the issuer. The all-time high was reached in 2000 (around $460/share). There is a triple bottom formed for around 50$/share.

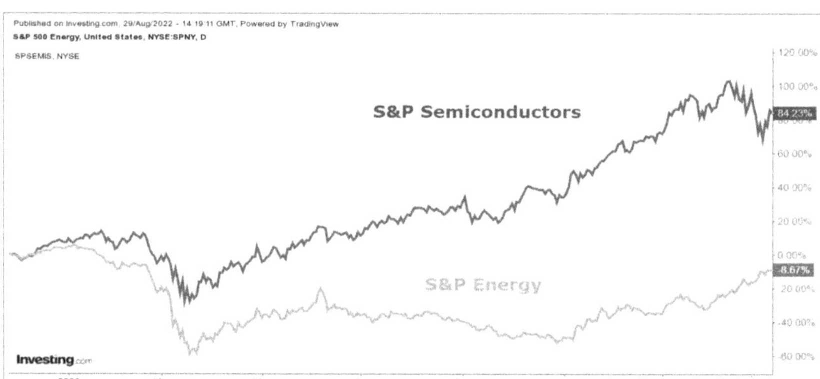

Fig. 4.17 Comparison of S&P energy and semiconductor indices, prior period (*Source* Chart from investing.com)

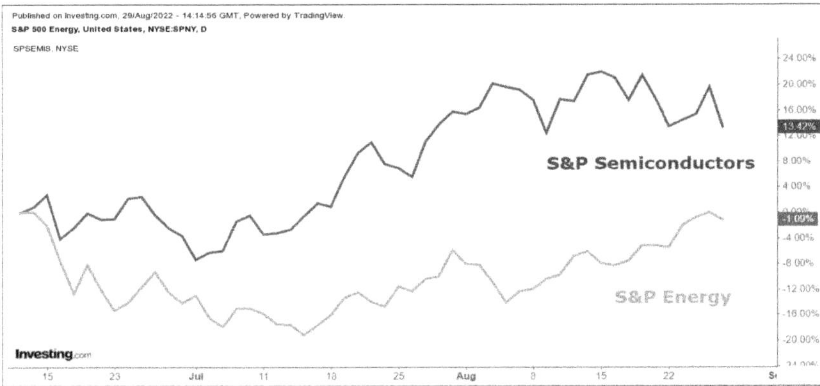

Fig. 4.18 Comparison of S&P energy and semiconductor indices, short investment horizon (*Source* Chart from investing.com)

What does this translate into? If you bought GE 22 years ago, the return on investment would have been around **−89%**. Bleak perspective isn't it?

But for anyone who followed the issuer closely, the $50/share level was an excellent buy point.

Fig. 4.19 General Electric evolution (*Source* Chart from investing.com)

September 2020–March 2021 in 7 months the return was **100%**. It illustrates that in the stock market, and especially based on technical analysis, you can win regardless of the fundamentals if the logic is based only on market realities and not on preconceived ideas. Of course, it is difficult to buy on almost absolute lows and sell on (intermediate) highs but it brings a solid perspective on the relativity of the investment process and especially the importance of the timing of the investment decision.

Buy a stock for 22 years and lose **89%**.

Buy a stock (the same) for 7 months and gain **100%**.

Moral of the story: do not disregard a stock just because it is on a downtrend. One beauty of the stock market is that you never know where the opportunities will pop up.

4.5 Finis Coronat Opus

Classical technical analysis uses charts to explain past price movements and forecast their future development. In a general sense, technical analysis uses historical data to intuit future trends; despite the caveat on any issue prospectus: "past performance does not guarantee future results".

But it should not be forgotten that technical analysis cannot be used on its own. Leaving aside the folklore that a mathematician randomly generated a chart, which then prompted a technical analyst to strongly recommend buying that non-existent stock. To give a more mundane example: log on to chartgame.com and try to beat, based on technical analysis alone, the simple buy and hold strategy. We believe that even the best analyst won't achieve much: without knowing the company, without knowing the period (macrocontext), and without having a comparable, the chances of success are minimal.

In summary, use the knowledge of technical analysis that follows in this book, but necessarily in conjunction with information from related areas, also suggested below.

Computers should also be used judiciously. At the beginning of the subprime crisis, automated systems were stopped from selling, lest profits fall. The falls and rebounds of hundreds (thousands) of points a day are also being made by computers. Even at reputable and considered safe firms, we find wrong data, unreliable, out-of-date quotes, or crashes at key moments. No program has yet been found that is always a winner or that is applicable to any security in any situation. This is both an impetus in research and a motivation to outperform the average market—stock market indices.

Note

1. https://markets.businessinsider.com/news/stocks/euro-2020-cristiano-ronaldo-coca-cola-market-value-snubs-drink-2021-6-1030526880.

References

Amin, S. (2021). The relationship between ethnic diversity and stock market development: A global perspective. In K. Jajuga & H. Locarek-Junge (Eds.), *Contemporary trends and challenges in finance*. Springer.

Brandimarte, P. (2018). *An introduction to financial markets—A quantitative approach*. Wiley.

Gavrilov, A. (2015). *Interaction and correlation between stock index prices and currency exchange rates*. Artyon Gavrilov Publishing.

Kuznetsov, A. (2006). *The complete guide to capital markets for quantitative professionals*. McGraw-Hill.

Schabacker, R. W. (2020). *Technical analysis and stock market profits* (Harriman definitive ed.) Harriman House.

Schwartz, R. A., Byrne, J. A., & Stempel, E. (2017). *Rapidly changing securities markets*. Springer.

Simmons, M. (2002). *Securities operations. A guide to trade position management*. Wiley.

Singh, S., & Yadav, S. S. (2021). *Security analysis and portfolio management. A primer*. Springer.

Strumeyer, G., & Swammy, S. (2017). *The capital markets: Evolution of the financial ecosystem*. Wiley Finance Series. Wiley.

Suangtho, S. (2012). *International stock portfolio and market correlations*. Lap Lambert Academic Publishing.

CHAPTER 5

Important Graphic Elements Used in Technical Analysis

Abstract These are the main elements of technical analysis. All will be made explicit and exemplified on domestic and foreign markets. We will show situations where the signals were false, and we will try predictions that can be verified in the future. We will try to answer the question: "is technical analysis a self-sustaining theory?" If all analysts, brokers, journalists, and investors notice that a declining pattern is forming and comment on it, few will likely buy at those times. Naturally, the price will decrease, due to the pressure on the sale side. The pattern will be confirmed in this way, concluding that technical analysis is a powerful method of stock market analysis. Could this be the explanation for the success of the technical analysis? Each pattern has an explanation. We will look at both their confirmations and their refutations in practice.

Keyword Main elements · Internal and external markets · Predictions · Brokers and investors · Patterns

One of the most important works in the field is Murphy's (1999) studies in which the author makes a comprehensive study of the soundness, methods, and applicability of technical analysis. Subsequently, other

F. C. Dumiter and F. M. Turcaş, *Technical Analysis Applications*,
https://doi.org/10.1007/978-3-031-27416-9_5

authors, such as Lo et al. (2000), show that technical analysis has a subjective character with respect to price-enriched geometric figures in historical charts.

Technical analysis should be evaluated within unbiased pattern recognition techniques and algorithms (Tsinaslanidis & Zapranis, 2016). Fong (2014) reveals some important aspects of a successful investment process as behavioral motivations and aspects and techniques of the Lotery Mindset. Other authors such as Schabacker (2005) present technical analysis as an integrated technique with several features such as support and resistance zones, trends, formations, and patterns, meanwhile McMillan (2017) suggests the importance of the movement of the price of an asset with a specific and complex analysis. Willey (2019) points out that short-term reform in financial markets is absolutely necessary due to legal and economic issues.

Di Lorenzo (2013) argues for a more comprehensive technical analysis agenda, with a special focus oriented upon Elliott wave theory and Gann charts. According to Chen (2010), technical analysis should encompass all essential and important methods and approaches, keeping abreast of the latest trends and models. Linton (2010) reviews the Ichimoku technique, interpreting, and further developing Cloud charts for professionals and investors.

It is easy to see that no stock market development is linear. Even the strongest trend is not strictly upward or downward; it has steeper or more hesitant upward or downward stretches, but it never just consists of consecutive daily gains (or losses) (Fig. 5.1).

Look at the evolution of the market at the beginning of the pandemic. Everyone was scared, total lockdown worldwide, and no one knew how we were going to get out of this situation. The market went in free-fall: companies did not know how and when they would be able to resume production; most speculators saw no prospect of keeping stocks in place of liquidity. No good news, quite the contrary. And yet, the market had days of rebounding (denoted by the green arrow, ascending ↗).

These momentary comebacks could not avoid the general decline. But the conclusion remains: even the strongest trend is not strictly upward or downward; it has steeper or more hesitant upward or downward stretches, but it never just consists of consecutive daily gains (or losses).

Fig. 5.1 Examples of minor moves opposing the main trend (*Source* Chart realized using the investing.com platform)

5.1 Trend Lines

5.1.1 Trend Lines Go Through Lows to Uptrends and Highs to Downward Trends

Let's consider the major (multi-year) trend of the S&P500, one of the most important indexes of the US market. It is noted that the price is permanently maintained above the trend line /. A brief intersection will be defined as a false signal—we must bear in mind that the market does not react mathematically, in unison, but there may be moments of irrationality.

This explains why the upward trend line goes through the lows: the end signal of the trend is the passing of the price below the trend line. In the following graph, the end of the decline is the breakdown of the minor downward trend line, figured in red \. We note again that it is not enough to simply intersect the trend line: for a trend to be considered over, it is necessary that the prices remain consistently on the other side of the trend line (Figs. 5.2 and 5.3).

Trends are major (multi-year), minor (daily or even shorter), and intermediate. A strong major trend usually has several subtrends, either in the direction of the major trend or opposite to it (Fig. 5.4).

Fig. 5.2 Ascending trend (*Source* Chart realized using the investing.com platform)

Fig. 5.3 Example of a downward trend (*Source* Chart realized using the investing.com platform)

As a good stock market advertisement, the multi-century trend is upward, which can be seen on the logarithmic chart of the oldest US market index, the Dow Jones Industrial. The logarithmic graph is linear, which means that the DJIA has exponential growth. We leave it to future

Fig. 5.4 Trends and subtrends (major and minor trends) (*Source* Chart realized using the investing.com platform)

generations of readers of this book to see if this is possible: by the end of the century, it should exceed 1,000,000 points (i.e. $)! (Fig. 5.5).

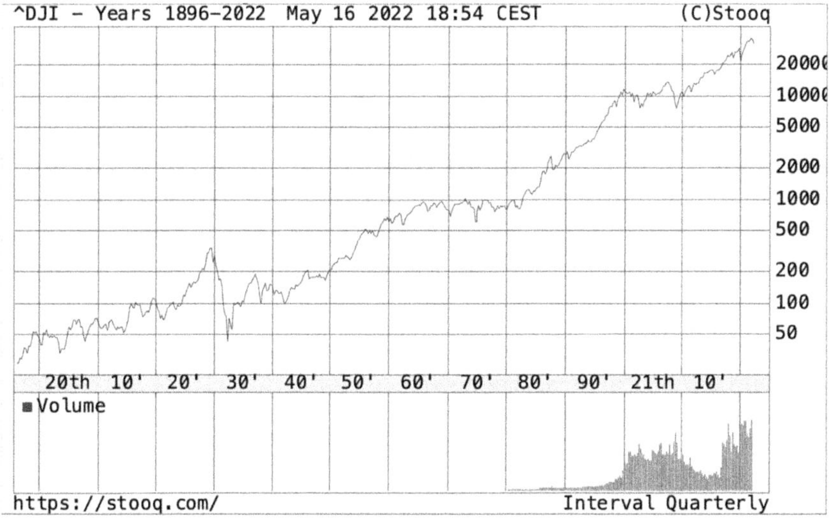

Fig. 5.5 Dow Jones historical logarithmic chart (*Source* stooq.com)

Fig. 5.6 Channel (*Source* Chart realized using the investing.com platform)

More powerful than a simple trend, trading channels also provide information on expected maximum increases/decreases. Please note that we are not looking for perfect charts for illustration. Technical analysis, like the stock market itself, is not a perfect machine, and it is better that way: otherwise, all readers of this book would become millionaires and would not buy other books (Fig. 5.6).

Price channels are very interesting because they allow for medium-lasting maneuvers. For example, in the situation presented in Fig. 5.7, speculators can predict that TEL will again reach the bottom line of the highlighted red down channel, so they can try taking a short position; after that, a rebound is expected, so they can take a long position.

5.2 Resistance, Support. Interchangeable Roles

We often naturally ask the question: decline, but what is the limit?

One possible answer can be given by the support line: the horizontal line that passes through several lows.

The explanation is simple: this is a threshold at which, in the past, investors have seen an opportunity to enter the market, thus exerting buying pressure. Well, if the support has been held in the past, it is expected that the next downward move will not breach it (Fig. 5.8).

Fig. 5.7 Well-defined descending channel (*Source* Chart realized using the bvb.ro platform)

Fig. 5.8 Support line (*Source* Chart realized using the investing.com platform)

Similar are the resistance lines: the price chart can't exceed a certain upward limit (Fig. 5.9).

Interestingly, often the same line turns from support to resistance and vice versa; they change roles (Fig. 5.10).

Fig. 5.9 Resistance line (*Source* Chart realized using the investing.com platform)

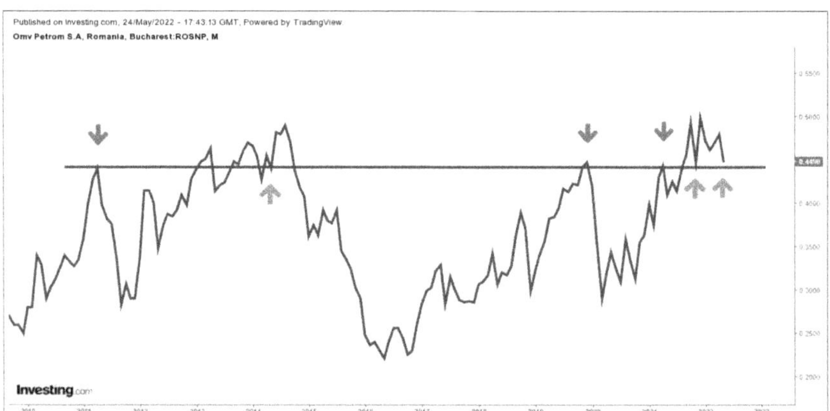

Fig. 5.10 Support and resistance changing their roles (*Source* Chart realized using the investing.com platform)

Unfortunately, this is not a universal rule; it is also possible to draw several supports/resistances without being able to specify which one is the most fitting. In the S&P500 chart in Fig. 5.10, many support/resistance lines can be drawn in an attempt to predict where the current decline ends (Fig. 5.11).

In this context, we also recall the theory according to which the prices that we see now, will be seen in the future also. Based on the idea that gaps are closing, this theory can predict the extent of price movements.

During the pandemic, Transgaz SA's stock price fell sharply on the Bucharest Stock Exchange, recording jumps—price ranges at which there were no transactions. The future evolution covered these gaps: just as nature does not like discontinuities, the human activities do not enjoy these ruptures of the charts either (Fig. 5.12).

Again, these considerations are not absolute: in the case of strong trends, gaps may appear that cannot be filled later. But usually, the market does not leave gaps. In the S&P500 chart, it is observed that regardless of the market direction (upward or downward), there are no gaps—strong movements are encircled in blue. In rare situations, the movement is so decided that there are price ranges in which no transactions take place. You have an example of an exhaustion gap covered and an initial gap

Fig. 5.11 Support/resistance lines are not absolute predictors (*Source* Chart realized using the investing.com platform)

Fig. 5.12 Gaps—part 1 (*Source* Chart realized using the investing.com platform)

(which must be closely watched and will very likely be covered when the market turns/rebounds) (Fig. 5.13).

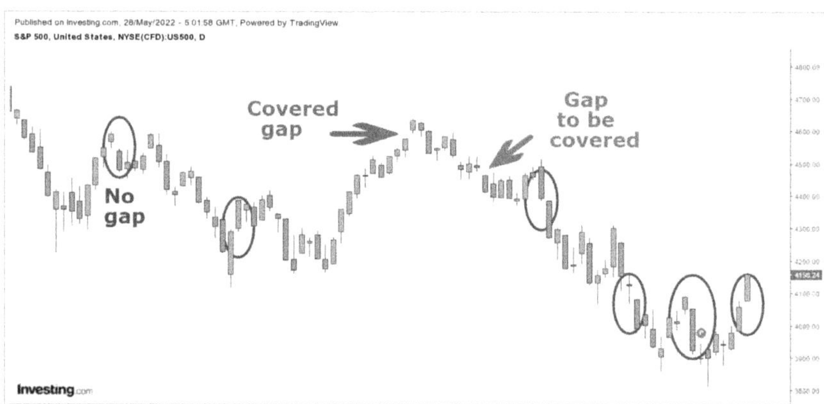

Fig. 5.13 Gaps—part 2 (*Source* Chart realized using the investing.com platform)

Fig. 5.14 Descending trend is confirmed by decreasing volume (*Source* Chart realized using the bvb.ro platform)

5.3 Volume

Volume is an important indicator for confirming or refuting market trends. Small amounts offered for trading (low volumes) can be a prerequisite for market manipulation. Obviously, this can only happen in underdeveloped markets or for under-traded issuers. However, these are exceptions in mature markets, so we will not focus on them here.

We will say that volume confirms the trend if it has the same direction as the change in the stock price; otherwise, we have a divergence, which denotes the weakness of the trend (Figs. 5.14 and 5.15).

As we will see, the volume plays an important role in certain patterns, especially in the famous head-and-shoulders.

5.4 Trend Continuation Patterns

We have shown that trends are not uniform in increasing or decreasing; they come in the form of fluctuations—some stronger, others weaker—often forming smaller waves in a large wave. The question therefore arises:

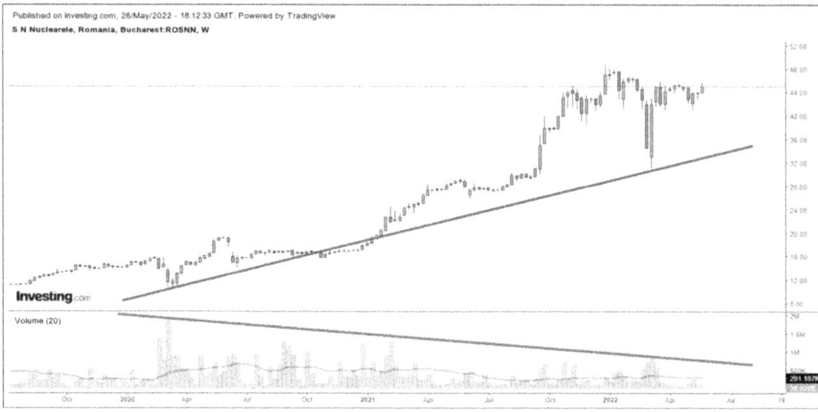

Fig. 5.15 Stock price—Volume divergence (*Source* Chart realized using the investing.com platform)

how do we know (or at least intuit) whether a movement contrary to the main trend constitutes a change in trend or just a brief relaxation of the main movement?

Patterns are the ones that indicate the continuation or the reverse of the trend.

The most well-known formation for continuing the trend is the ascending triangle (within the upward trend) (Fig. 5.16).

Triangles can be found on downward trends too.

Also, there may be specific formations (wedges, flags, pennants) that behave similarly to triangles.

5.5 Reverse Patterns

The most interesting reverse pattern is head-and-shoulders.

The stock price goes up in large volume to a certain level (the left shoulder), then retreats. It grows again, to an equal or higher level (the head), on even greater volume, then again decreases (right shoulder). Finally, with one last attempt, it increases but fails to overcome the previous limits, then falls below the level of the shoulders (the neckline).

Why is this a pattern? Our explanation is that it's self-confirming. Once the head-and-shoulders signals appear, the brokers, the analysts, the press, and the public observe them and rushes to report them. Investors will be

Fig. 5.16 In an upward trend, BET forms an ascending triangle (*Source* Chart realized using the investing.com platform)

reluctant to buy again, waiting for things to calm down; panicked people will sell thinking that a drop is coming. Thus, the mere appearance of the signals will lead to the confirmation of a pattern that, in itself, probably would not have said anything if it was not advertised.

For example, EVER on the Romanian market has no reasons to engage on a bearish path. The readers will confirm or not if the obvious head-and-shoulders pattern observed in Fig. 5.17 will be followed by a downward movement or if the investors will neglect this technical pattern.

A more realistic reverse pattern is a double (or triple, or multiple) top (or bottom). This has a more logical explanation: the price cannot exceed a certain value, because at this value the sellers exit, and the buyers are reluctant to enter the market. So, temporarily, the upward trend is reversed until it gains momentum and surpasses the resistance line.

In Fig. 5.18, we note that the Procter & Gamble stock could not pass \$165 at the beginning of 2022, thus creating a multiple top and leading to a reverse of the upward trend. The comeback at the beginning of May

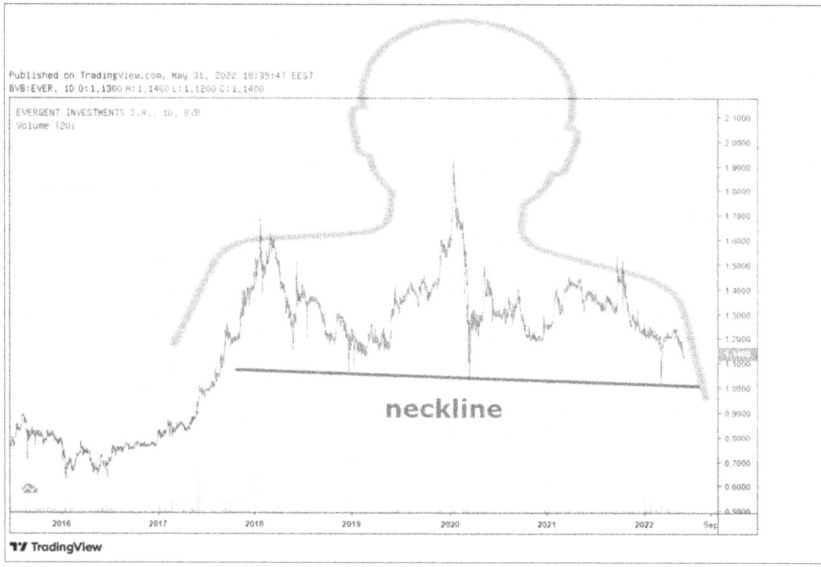

Fig. 5.17 Head-and-shoulders pattern (*Source* Chart generated on the invest ing.com platform)

2022 could not exceed that threshold either so a resistance was born, represented with the blue line in Fig. 5.18.

5.6 Fibonacci Retracements and Extensions

Fibonacci numbers are frequently found in nature and come from the series $x_n = x_{n-2} + x_{n-1}$, with $x_0 = 0$ and $x_1 = 1$. We retrieve the Fibonacci ratios in snail spirals, tree branches, and ideal proportions of human faces. Being so common in nature, the numbers have found their correspondence on the stock market as well, in the form of Fibonacci extensions and retracements.

Figure 5.19 shows that the market began to decline in February 2022, with the Russian invasion of Ukraine. Although the outcome of the war could not be predicted, the question for investors was "to what extent are stock prices likely to fall?". As we have seen, it is likely to stop at resistance or previous support; but at which one, because there are many such limits that can be plotted on the chart? Fibonacci retracements provide a

Fig. 5.18 Multiple top (*Source* Chart realized using the investing.com platform)

possible answer, especially for large declines: at one of the limits of 32.8%, 50% (this is not a Fibonacci number, but it is an important psychological marker), 61.8% or even 100%, all linked to the previous uptrend. And we see that the decline stopped near the first Fibonacci line.

Similarly, the question arises for the upside: from historical highs on an uptrend, what might be the most important resistance? Here, other patterns or indicators don't give us any information: they will only react when approaching the peak. However, Fibonacci extensions can outline these future thresholds. In Fig. 5.20, we can see that after a decrease in the upward trend, the subsequent growth stopped at the Fibonacci line of 50%.

And here we must emphasize that Fibonacci constructions are not absolutely certain mathematics: the starting point and the selection of the line of interest are matters that depend on the analyst. Obviously, there are Fibonacci structures that are more reliable than others and more strongly outlined. But the fact that they are relative makes them difficult to implement as a precise mathematical analysis.

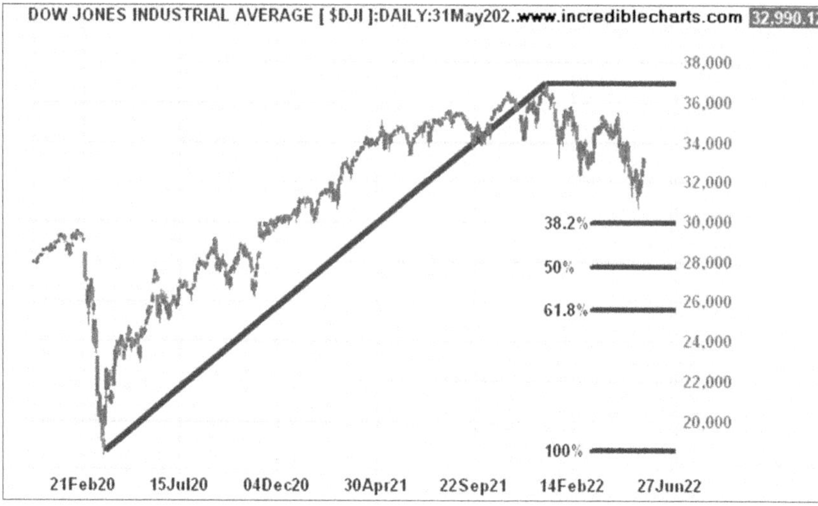

Fig. 5.19 Fibonacci retracements (*Source* Chart realized using the incrediblech arts.com software)

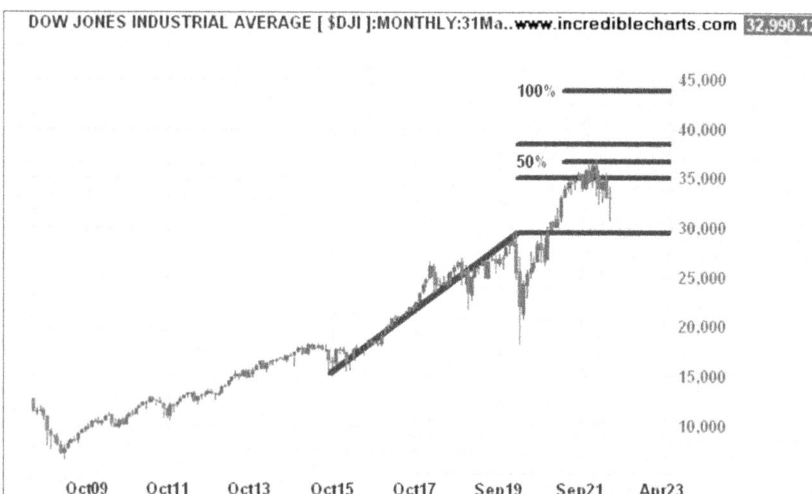

Fig. 5.20 Fibonacci extensions (*Source* Chart realized using the incrediblech arts.com software)

5.7 Elliott Wave

Elliott wave is a very known and highly popular (see the websites included in the reference section) method of dividing the chart of a traded stock into impulsive, wave, and corrective phase. The impulsive phase consists of 5 alternating successive movements and the corrective phase of 3 such movements. After the big movement (super-cycle) is shaped, every part can be subdivided into smaller Elliott waves.

Why 5 and 3? Because these are the smallest numbers with which theory can work!

Obviously, there are conditions regarding the duration and extent of each phase, the limits to which it can be extended, and even conditions in which these rules can be breached (Fig. 5.21).

After dividing big waves into smaller waves, you may obtain a complicated image of the phase where the market is (Fig. 5.22).

We are not fans of this type of analysis for 2 main reasons:

- In fact, it is never known which wave we are on, at all the moments; most analyses specify at least two possibilities of framing in the theory.

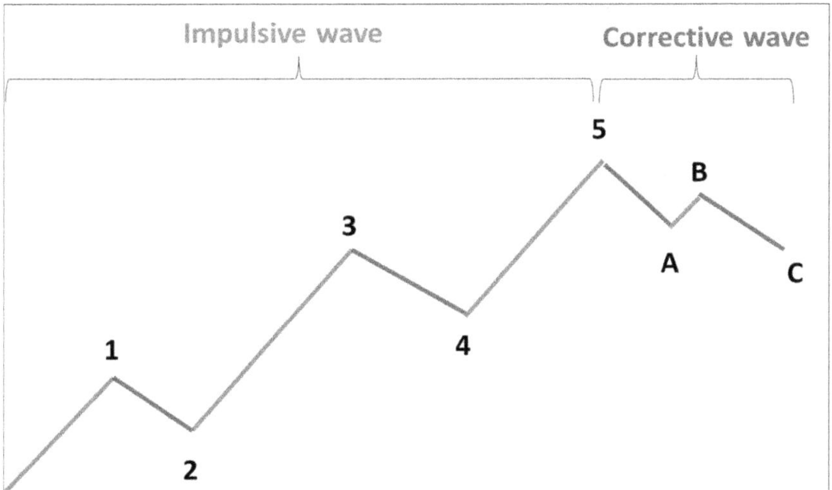

Fig. 5.21 Theoretical Elliott wave (*Source* Own design)

Fig. 5.22 Example of Elliott wave analysis (*Source* https://elliottwavestreet.com/elliott-wave/elliott-wave-eurusd-under-jackson-hole-pressure/)

- On the big picture, the Elliott wave highlight is forced, in fact, not even the super-cycle fits into theory, much less the secondary waves.

As an example, find the Elliott wave on DJIA index multiannual Fig. 5.23 chart, considering that (Murphy, 1999):

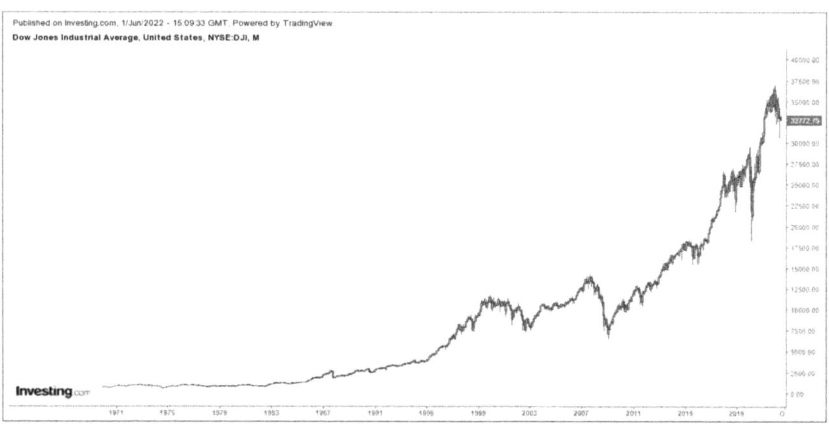

Fig. 5.23 DJIA grand cycle (*Source* Chart realized using the incrediblecharts.com software)

- Every advancing (impulse) wave must have 5 subphases; every corrective wave must have exactly only 3.
- If one impulsive wave extends, the other 2 must be equal in time and value.
- Downward movement should not extend under the previous low.
- Wave 4 should not overlap wave 1.
- The theory works better in indexes than in individual stocks.

It's obvious we can easily find a lot of different waves, but hardly Elliott ones.

5.8 Point and Figure Charts

Point and figure charts work on a different principle than point charts: here it is not time that matters, only the direction of the market.

The chart is composed of columns of ascending Xs and descending 0 s. Each time the price moves above a certain predetermined level, an x is placed over the current column of xs. When the trend reverses, the column of x's is dropped and a 0 is placed in the next column to the right, which is made up only of 0's, starting one position below the previous x. When the trend reverses, the column of 0's is resumed and a new column of x's is opened on the right, one level above the last 0.

In Fig. 5.24, let us observe that the horizontal axis has no meaning: the April month is longer than the whole of the 2020 year. Then let's notice that each x column begins over the last 0 columns and each 0 column begins under the last x column. This means that at every reverse we lose a tempo because we have no means to determine in advance the market turnaround. Finally, every column of ascending x's or descending 0's can bring us profit, if we stay on the right side of the market.

So, the strategy implied is quite simple: we must adopt a long position when the chart is on x columns and a short position when we are in 0. The gain/loss is determined by counting the symbols in the same column, minus 2 (losses due to the delay of the reversal of the investment position due to the trend change), which is then multiplied by the range of variation (the vertical distance between each x and each 0 in any column).

In strong trends, we will win, in the trading market or rapidly changing one we will lose.

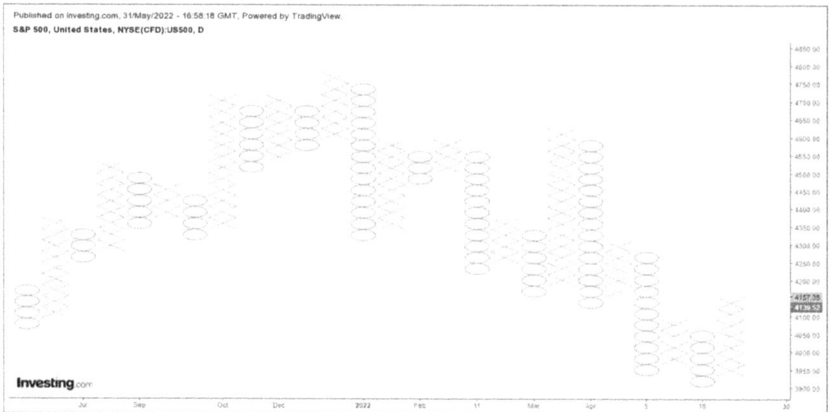

Fig. 5.24 Point and figures chart (*Source* Chart realized using the investing.com platform)

In this type of chart is very important to correctly choose the parameters: the box size (the interval in which we put another sign on the columns) and the reversal amount (how much we attend until we consider the reversal done) (Fig. 5.25).

Let's try to apply the discussed methods to an actual chart. The conclusions can be verified by readers in the near future. We will analyze the DJIA index, created by summing up the stock prices of 30 of the American blue chips.

On the monthly chart, it can be seen that the general trend is an upward one, which is visible on the logarithmic chart.

The weekly chart shows both the ascending channel in which it was enrolled after the subprime crisis and the false breakdown caused by the pandemic.

The daily chart shows a flag, a formation that signals a brief stop on the upward trend, which must briefly resume. We would have expected the drop to end below, at the Fibonacci retreat of 38.2%, the limit that also represented a strong previous resistance and even a gap. In fine, the point chart and figures confirm the period of high volatility, in which speculators feel at ease and investors would do better to wait for calmer times (Fig. 5.26).

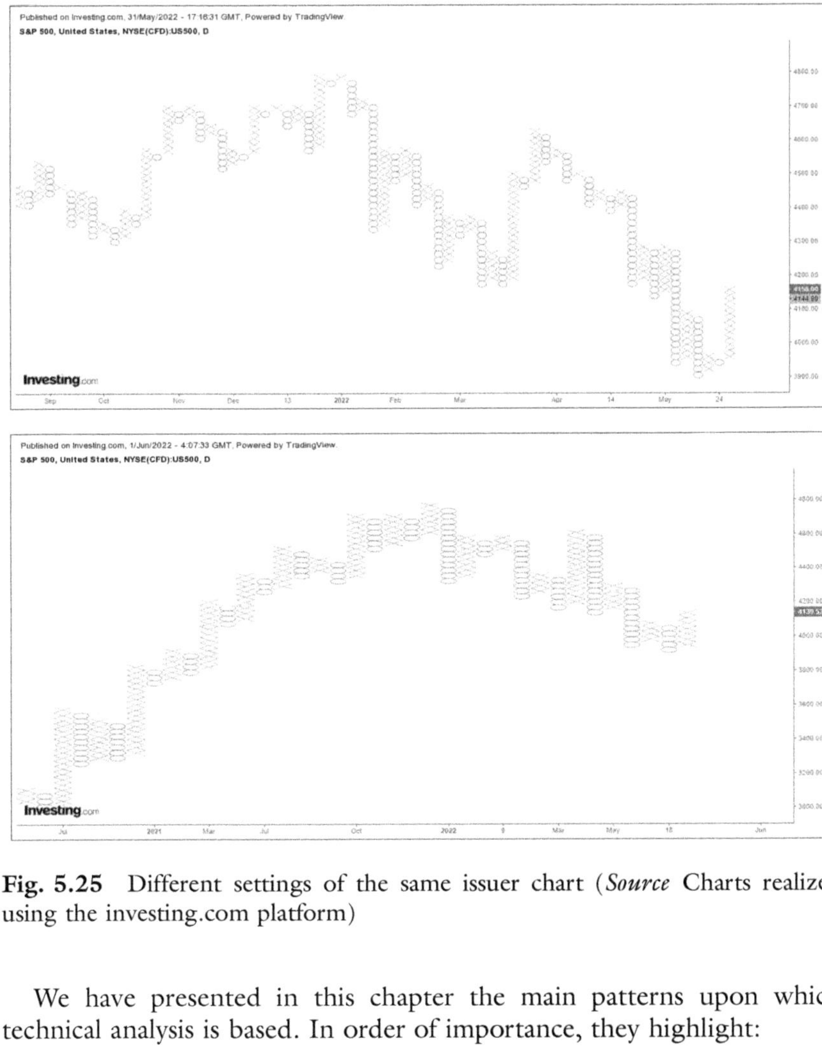

Fig. 5.25 Different settings of the same issuer chart (*Source* Charts realized using the investing.com platform)

We have presented in this chapter the main patterns upon which technical analysis is based. In order of importance, they highlight:

1. The trend we are on (or the channel in which the stock price fits).
2. The limits to which the movements are expected, especially those of reversion: resistance and support.
3. Patterns affected during the trend: continuation, respectively reverse.

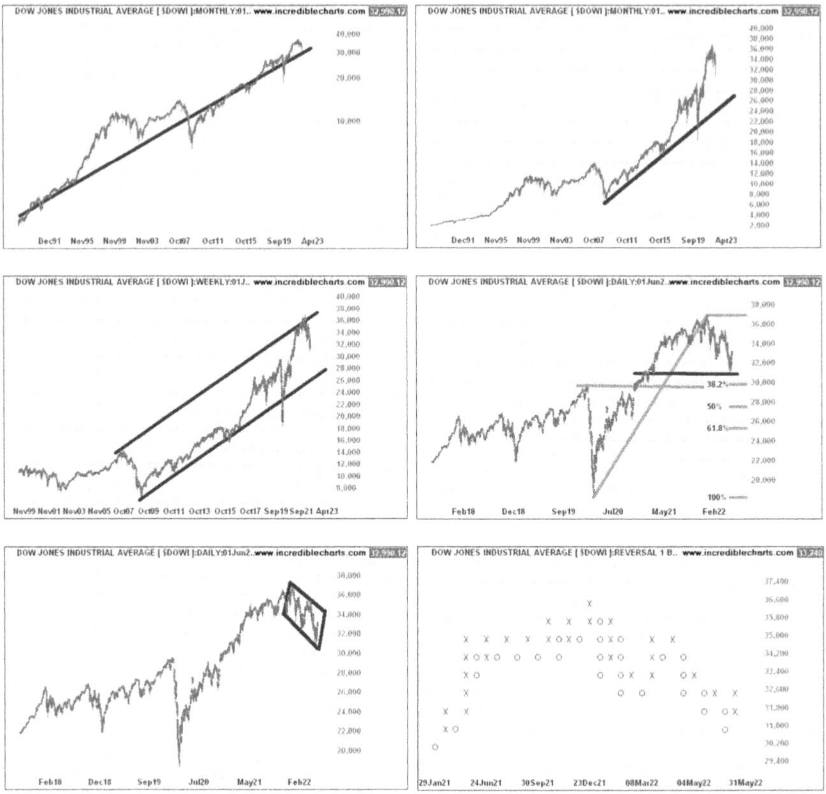

Fig. 5.26 DJIA technical analysis: patterns (*Source* Chart realized using the inc rediblecharts.com software Finis Coronat Opus)

Fibonacci extensions and retracements, Elliott wave—signals about where we are and where we are going.

References

Chen, J. (2010). *Essentials of technical analysis for financial markets*. John Wiley and Sons, Inc.

Di Lorenzo, R. (2013). *Basic technical analysis of financial markets*. Springer.

Fong, W. (2014). *The lottery mindset: Investors, gambling and the stock market*. Palgrave Macmillan.

https://elliottwave-forecast.com/elliott-wave-theory/
https://tradingelliottwave.com/
https://wavechart.com/
https://www.e-wavecharts.com/
Linton, D. (2010). *Trading success with the Ichimoku technique*. British Library.
Lo, A., Mamaysky, H., Wang, J. (2000). Foundation of technical analysis: Computational algorithms, statistical inference and empirical implementation, *NBER Working Paper No. w7613*, pp. 1–37.
McMillan, D. (2018). *Predicting stock returns—implications for asset prices*. Palgrave Macmillan.
Murphy, J.J. (1999). *Technical analysis of the financial markets. A comprehensive guide to trading methods and applications*. New York Institute of Finance.
Schabacker, R. (2005). *Technical analysis and stock market profits: The real bible of technical analysis*. Harriman House, Ltd.
Tsinaslanidis, P., & Zapranis, A. (2016). *Technical analysis for algorithm pattern recognition*. Springer.
Willey, K. (2019). *Stock market short-termism*. Palgrave Macmillan.

CHAPTER 6

Indicators and Oscillators Used in Technical Analysis

Abstract We will briefly mention other indicators. We remind you that there are over 100 such indicators and oscillators; some can be customized (as parameters). We will look in detail at the ones that are, in our opinion, the most relevant. However, we are interested in answering the following questions: What are indicators? What are oscillators? What do they tell us? How can we use them? Simple charts are not enough to try to predict trend changes or the strength of trends. In fact, these are the most important questions: will the bearish (bullish) market continue? Will the trend reverse? Where is the action heading? Trend strength, change signals, and market momentum are decisive in investments/development decisions.

Keyword Indicators · Oscillators · Trend changes · Signals · Momentum of the market

An important feature of the global economy is based upon the comprehensive studies and practical cases developed by Pring (2014), which hypothesizes that the only thing that determines price in securities is people's evolving perception of emerging fundamentals, while the authors analyze and highlight the most important trends in the investment process in this era of innovative investment and complex techniques. Other specialists have produced insightful practical guides *vis-à-vis* indicators,

F. C. Dumiter and F. M. Turcaş, *Technical Analysis Applications*,
https://doi.org/10.1007/978-3-031-27416-9_6

oscillators, and market conditions in a well-complex handbook (Achelis, 2014).

An interesting study deals with the interviews with top money-makers and specialists regarding the establishment of sequential steps of the super trader's successful agenda (Schwager, 2012). Kirkpatrick and Dahlquist (2016) reveal a series of techniques such as risk mitigation, sentiment indices, momentum indicators, and flow of funds in order to establish some interesting investment paths and strategies for the stock market.

Bulkowski (2021) establishes an important work oriented toward stock markets and financial footprints; the complex work of the author reveals some important features of chart patterns, special quirks, and trading busted patterns. Nison (2001) assesses an important study regarding Japanese candlestick charts revealing some important new techniques and skills for future development of the traders' and investors' strategies of the stock market.

Rockefeller (2014) debates and discusses the fundamental importance of technical analysis regarding the trading decisions; this study is oriented toward a new way of important features used in technical analysis such as decisions regarding the usage of the real data, turning points, and portfolio performances. Other specialists such as Collins (2017) evaluate and assess the appliance of the Elliott Wave Principle by understating the sequences and steps for implementing this strategy. In the aftermath, Edwards and Magee (2021) made a comprehensive study dealing with fine-tuning aspects such as volume, primarily price, past data studies, and forecasting the prices; the authors adopt in this study contradictory opinions regarding modern portfolio theory.

6.1 Moving Averages

We have seen that trends end where the trend line is breached; sometimes, however, this intersection is short-lived, resulting in a false breakout. However, it is not the pattern that signals the power of the trend, but the momentum.

In Fig. 6.1, we see that as time goes by, we can draw numerous trend lines, starting from the April 2020 low (the end of the decline caused by the pandemic) and intersecting relative lows (increasingly higher in value).

But nothing tells us which of these intersections really signals a change in trend. This is where the first indicators come in: moving averages. These are averages (arithmetic or exponential) of prices, calculated taking

Fig. 6.1 A lot of the trend line breaches on the S&P500 chart (*Source* Chart created on investing.com)

into account only the most recent data: usually 50, 100, and 200 units of time: days, weeks, and months—Fig. 6.2.

The rule, on an uptrend, is that the moving averages should be in order of duration: the longest lower, the average higher, while the shortest is the highest. When these moving averages intersect and change positions it

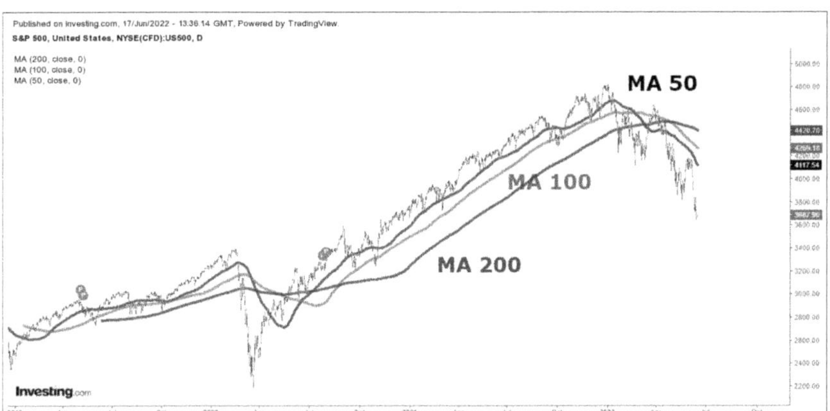

Fig. 6.2 Moving averages (*Source* Chart made on investing.com)

means that the upward trend weakens and signals a likely trend reversal. In Fig. 6.2, we see that in April 2022 the position of the averages reversed completely, signaling a strong downtrend, still in place at the time the chart was made.

6.2 Moving Average Convergence Divergence

MACD is another important indicator to judge the strength of the trend and the closeness of its reversal.

For this, the basic rule is that the trend is probable to be reversed if a "beak" is formed, in the sense that the shorter average (in the upward trends) goes below the longer average (or vice versa, in the downward trends) (Fig. 6.3).

The use of the MACD depends largely on its parameter settings, which vary depending on the stock, index, or financial instrument chosen and even from analyst to analyst.

In Fig. 6.4, it can be observed that, although the major signals are similar, one setting shows much clearer trend changes but with some delay, while another setting is faster but gives many false signals (because the curves are much closer together).

Fig. 6.3 MACD (*Source* Chart processed on investing.com)

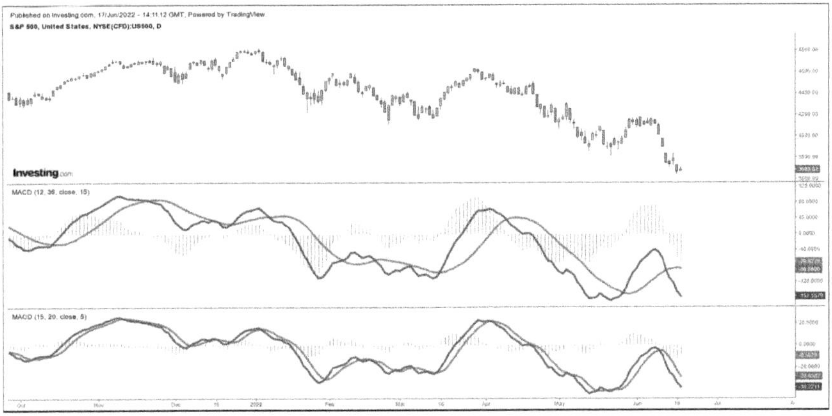

Fig. 6.4 MACD different parameter settings (*Source* Chart processed on investing.com)

6.3 Relative Strength Index

RSI is an oscillator: unlike indicators—which have numerical values linked to stock market movements—oscillators only take values in finite intervals: usually 0 ÷ 1 (0% ÷ 100%). RSI signals specific overbought (when it takes values above 70%) and oversold (below 30%) areas (Fig. 6.5).

Fig. 6.5 RSI (*Source* Chart elaborated on investing.com)

Here, attention should be drawn to a possible foolish phenomenon: apparent confirmation. When studying the trend and its changes we seek to rely not on a single argument, but on the different reasons that contribute to a common conclusion. For example, a mere touch of the trend line is not enough to consider that a reversal is coming; we also look at indicators, oscillators, patterns, and maybe even fundamentals of macroeconomic environments.

Well, RSI often tends to copy the shape of the stock chart, sometimes inducing a false confirmation: it increases with the increase in quotation (or vice versa). That is why the similarity of ticker and RSI graphs does not matter, only the position of the RSI and its trend of evolution.

6.4 Bollinger Bands

BB is drawn directly on the chart of the security and consists of a moving average curve, surrounded on either side by curves drawn (usually) at the $\pm 2\ \sigma$ (two standard deviations from the mean), named bands (Fig. 6.6).

It can be observed that the evolution of the security usually lies between these bands, and it is expected to oscillate between them. This is due to the fact that, in the case of the normal (Gaussian) distribution, only 5% of the cases in the statistical population lie outside the $\mu \pm 1.96\ \sigma$ range.

According to Turcaş et al. (2017), the return distribution (of daily gains/losses, expressed as a percentage) is not at all normal (Gaussian).

Fig. 6.6 Bollinger Bands (*Source* Chart created on investing.com)

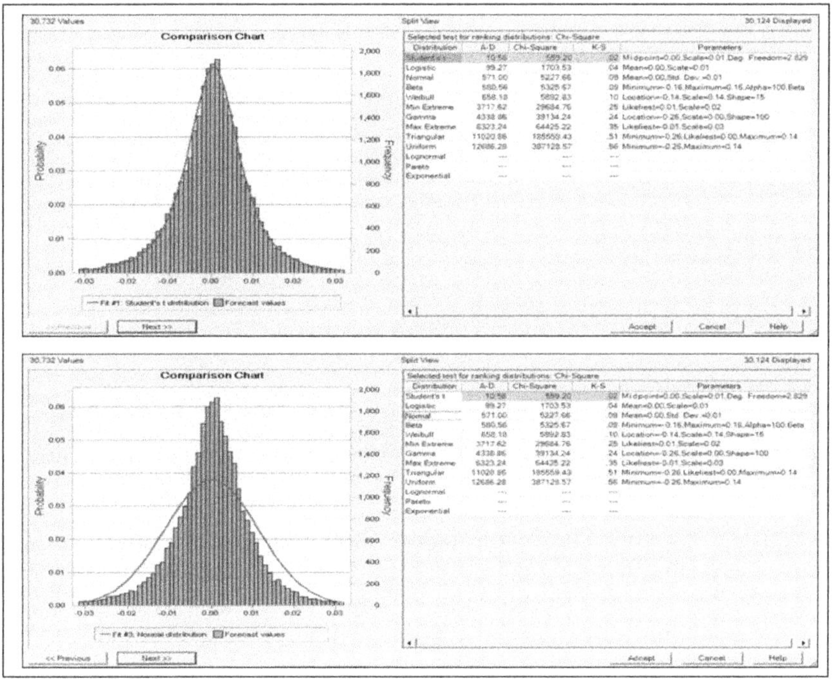

Fig. 6.7 Framing of daily returns in standardized distributions (*Source* Chart made in cristal ball [excel])

However, the deviation is not large, and the law of large numbers suggests that the natural tendency is to follow this distribution.

BB's interpretation is as follows: when they widen, the trend comes to an end and a change in follows. The BB width is therefore a signal of continuation (if the bands are close together) or of reversal of the trend (if they depart). Confirmation is provided in Fig. 6.8; unfortunately, however, there is no way to predict how much the bands will widen and when the widening will peak (Fig. 6.7).

6.5 Finis Coronat Opus

Indicators and oscillators are important because they are based on mathematical formulas and can therefore be easily implemented in automated

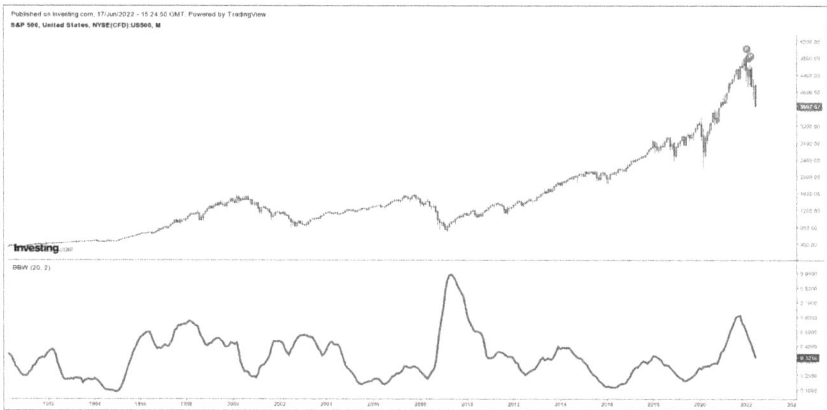

Fig. 6.8 Bollinger Band Width (*Source* Chart processed on investing.com)

computing systems. The image below shows that the technical projections offered by investing.com are based solely on these indicators and oscillators, calculated automatically for any given security (Fig. 6.9).

Combined, indicators, and oscillators can be good predicting tools for major trend confirmations/changes. On purpose, the examples presented refers to the same security, in order to conclude how these results can be assembled.

In Fig. 6.10 we can see that:

- From Fig. 6.2, it follows that the moving averages were positioned according to a secondary downward trend.
- The Bollinger Bands departed from each other strongly in April 2022 → the upward trend was finished. Now they tend to get closer because the secondary downward trend is in place.
- MACD made the beak down and shows no signs of recovery → the same conclusion: trend reversal, followed by a strong downward trend.
- RSI heading to the oversold area; until then, the downward trend is in force.

Again, it is interesting to see which of these forecasts come true and which do not, but especially to conclude how we should set and interpret the data in order to forecast as accurately as possible the next movements of the market.

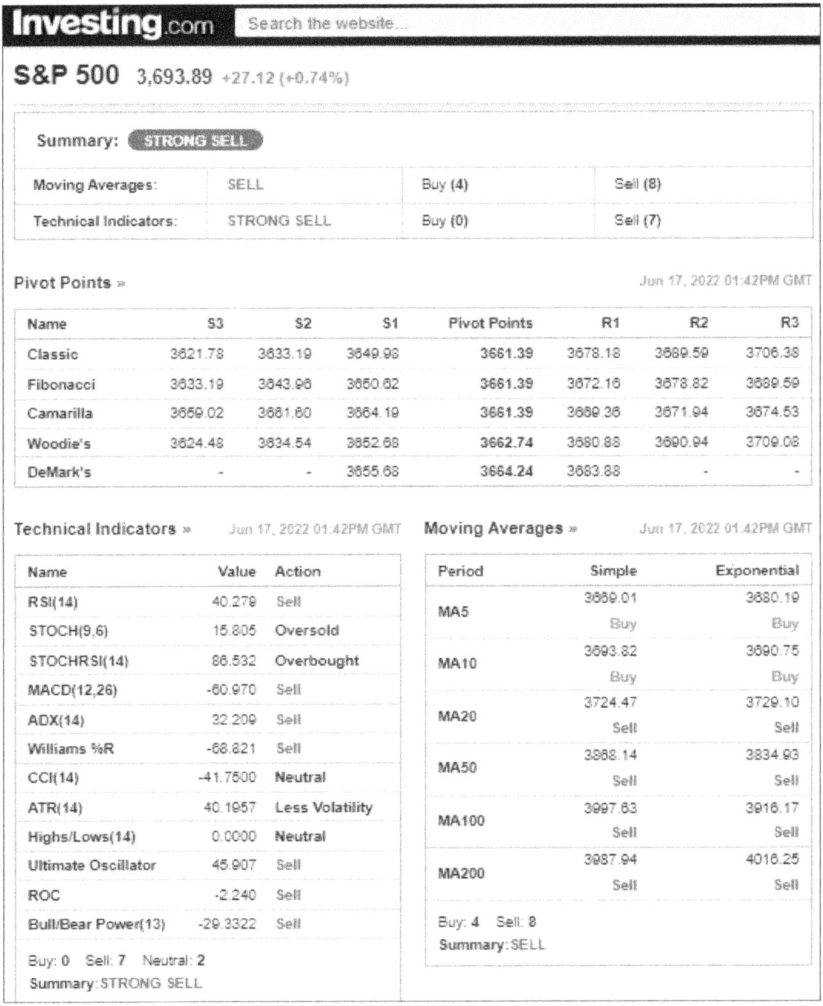

Investing.com Search the website...

S&P 500 3,693.89 +27.12 (+0.74%)

Summary: STRONG SELL

Moving Averages:	SELL	Buy (4)	Sell (8)
Technical Indicators:	STRONG SELL	Buy (0)	Sell (7)

Pivot Points » Jun 17, 2022 01:42PM GMT

Name	S3	S2	S1	Pivot Points	R1	R2	R3
Classic	3621.78	3633.19	3649.98	3661.39	3678.18	3689.59	3706.38
Fibonacci	3633.19	3643.96	3650.62	3661.39	3672.16	3678.82	3689.59
Camarilla	3659.02	3661.60	3664.19	3661.39	3669.36	3671.94	3674.53
Woodie's	3624.48	3634.54	3652.68	3662.74	3680.88	3690.94	3709.08
DeMark's	-	-	3655.68	3664.24	3683.88	-	-

Technical Indicators » Jun 17, 2022 01:42PM GMT

Name	Value	Action
RSI(14)	40.279	Sell
STOCH(9,6)	15.805	Oversold
STOCHRSI(14)	86.532	Overbought
MACD(12,26)	-60.970	Sell
ADX(14)	32.209	Sell
Williams %R	-68.821	Sell
CCI(14)	-41.7500	Neutral
ATR(14)	40.1957	Less Volatility
Highs/Lows(14)	0.0000	Neutral
Ultimate Oscillator	45.907	Sell
ROC	-2.240	Sell
Bull/Bear Power(13)	-29.3322	Sell

Buy: 0 Sell: 7 Neutral: 2
Summary: STRONG SELL

Moving Averages » Jun 17, 2022 01:42PM GMT

Period	Simple	Exponential
MA5	3669.01 Buy	3680.19 Buy
MA10	3693.82 Buy	3690.75 Buy
MA20	3724.47 Sell	3729.10 Sell
MA50	3868.14 Sell	3834.93 Sell
MA100	3997.63 Sell	3916.17 Sell
MA200	3987.94 Sell	4016.25 Sell

Buy: 4 Sell: 8
Summary: SELL

Fig. 6.9 Recommendations based on technical indicators (*Source* Screenshot from investing.com)

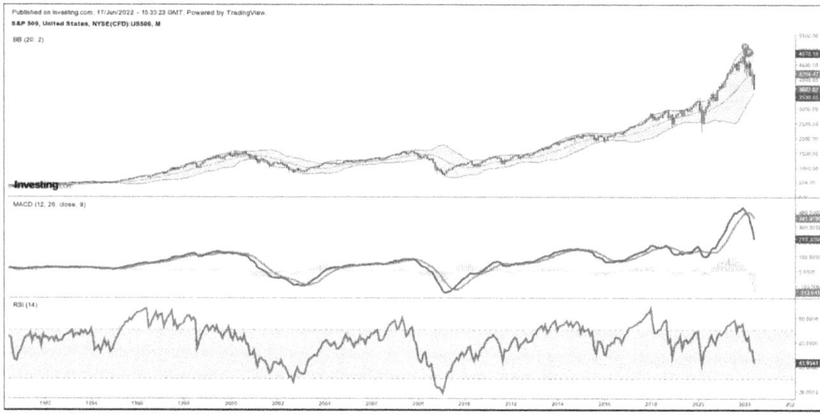

Fig. 6.10 S&P500 indicators and oscillators analyses (*Source* Chart processed on investing.com)

References

Achelis, S. B. (2014). *Technical analysis from A to Z*—2nd Edition. Mc Graw Hill.

Bulkowski, T. (2021). *Encyclopedia of chart patterns*— (3rd ed.). Wiley.

Collins, C. J. (2017). *Elliot wave principle: A key to market behavior*. New Classics Library.

Edwards, R. D., & Magee, J. (2021). *Technical analysis of stock trends*. New Publisher.

Kirkpatrick, C. D., & Dahlquist, J. R. (2016). *Technical analysis: The complete resource for financial market*—3rd Edition. FT Press.

Nison, S. (2001). *Japanese candlestick charting techniques: A contemporary guide to the ancient investment techniques of the far East*—2nd Edition. Pretince Hall Press.

Pring, M. J. (2014). *Technical analysis explained*—(5th ed.). McGraw Hill.

Rockefeller, B. (2014). *Technical analysis for dummies*— (3rd ed.). John Wiley & Sons.

Schwager, J. D. (2012). *Market wizards: Interviews with top traders*. Wiley.

Turcaş, F., Dumiter, F., Brezeanu, P., Fărcaş, P., & Coroiu, S. (2017). Practical aspects of portfolio selection and optimisation on the capital market. *Economic Research-Ekonomska Istrazivanja, 30*(1), 14–30.

CHAPTER 7

Stock Exchange Predictions

Abstract This chapter is not actually part of the technical analysis. It is our proposal to summarize the results of the full analysis in the form of estimating the chances of achieving certain values in the future. We will show that predictions about the evolution of securities cannot be made by brokerage houses, because they could be hedged by speculators. But to quote the probability of evolution is the most predictable tool that can be presented to an investor, instead of the traditional buy/sell or bull/bear.

Keywords Predictions · Securities · Brokerage houses · Speculators · Investor

Stock market forecasts and predictions represent an interesting domain that must be analyzed both theoretically and practically. Dumiter and Turcaş (2022) emphasize that there are several important theories that must be considered regarding the associated risk of the expected return on investment; moreover, regarding the practical aspects, the forecasting models must be further improved to enhance the soundness of the investment process.

Jimon et al. (2021) highlight that for an investment portfolio, the main importance has the financial instruments which are enriched in the investment funds on the investor. Turcaş et al. (2017) suggest that there is

F. C. Dumiter and F. M. Turcaş, *Technical Analysis Applications*,
https://doi.org/10.1007/978-3-031-27416-9_7

room to maneuver regarding the construction of an optimal and efficient portfolio.

Other authors reveal the great importance of modeling the financial markets, which is an essential aspect both for the financial industry and academia in the context of market revisions and prediction of market prices (Zheng & Chen, 2013). Brooks (2012) analyzes some important aspects for traders and investors regarding the usage of price action for establishing trade on the market.

The importance of advanced applied investments, asset allocation, and portfolio management is seen as a *quid pro quo* for practitioners and traders worldwide with a special focus oriented upon a symbiosis between academic approaches and best practice advice (Stewart et al., 2019).

Elton et al. (2014) discuss and debate the important problem of an optimal portfolio, along with types of input. The authors conclude that assessing the securities characteristics related to the investor's methods of portfolio computing sets is very important. Fabozzi et al. (2014) reveal the importance of econometric modeling related to finance in general, and related to the stock markets, especially, coming to the conclusion that it is very important for investors to evaluate and assess the proper econometric models related to portfolio allocation, volatility estimation, and capital asset.

A very interesting study is the one of Fabozzi and Markowitz (2011) in which the authors explain the complex investment management strategy process regarding the methods and investment practices, sophisticated investors thinking, and some unique techniques applied to the stock market. Subsequently, Pachamanova and Fabozzi (2010) evaluate and assess the importance of some interesting modeling techniques regarding the stock markets using several econometric software and techniques for academics and investors.

7.1 What Are Predictions? The Probability Behind Them

So far we have seen that approaches to capital markets are diverse and sometimes even contradictory. In the hope of determining how a single parameter—the share price—will evolve, the technical analysis starts from the only two parameters known from the past: price and trading volume. By considering geometric chart formations, dozens of indicators and oscillators, and complex statistical techniques or mathematical models, technical analysis attempts to predict future developments.

In contrast, the fundamental analysis starts from considerations of the company's market, its functions, and hundreds of financial parameters and ultimately concludes with the same investment decision: buy–hold–sell.

Modern methods investigate concepts such as machine learning, genetic algorithms, or econophysics. Here we should point out that refining mathematical methods do not necessarily bring an outstanding stock market result. Markets are not efficient, the interests of participants are varied, and the overall evolution depends on variables that are sometimes impossible to control. Higher accuracy of mathematical models and methods does not lead to more accurate results, as long as the human factor is not quantified. Engineers would quantify the accumulation of errors in this way: "*measure with a micrometer, draw with a chalk, cut with an axe*". Moreover, since markets are dynamically unstable, the principle of critical points applies to them: under conditions of unstable dynamic equilibrium, the flapping of the wings of a butterfly in Mexico can influence the behavior of a tornado in the Midwest.

Behavioral analysis is even more difficult to perform because the investment profile of the multitude of market participants is unknown. And although most trades in mature markets are executed by machines (automated trading systems), psychological considerations are very important both as a herd spirit and as a decision to use computer programs because no algorithm can be equally efficient in rising, stagnant, or declining markets, in volatile or anemic markets, in securities with different liquidity or free float.

And valuation approaches, while supposed to help the investment decision, can only determine the value of the company as a whole, without contributing much to the calculation of market capitalization.

That leaves one area that should be addressed, that of probabilities. The layman's argument would be the use in everyday life of specific expressions: "what are the chances of … "; 'what are the odds of'. A more doctrinal reason would be the International Valuation Standards IVS provision: «*…note that when a probability-weighted expected cash flow is used, it is not always necessary for valuers to take into account distributions of all possible cash flows using complex models and techniques. Rather, valuers may develop a limited number of discrete scenarios and probabilities that capture the array of possible cash flows…*»

Because the basic mathematical formula: number of favorable cases over the number of total possible cases is not applicable, we naturally turn to subjective probabilities.

The probability of these scenarios is subjective, yet based on experience and professional reasoning (Dumiter & Turcaş, 2022).

Subjective probabilities can be defined as the degree of confidence. They are equivalent to the amount a player would be willing to invest in a YES or NO bet with odds of 1. As a principle, the final probabilities follow the next rules:

- No Dutch book: additivity of independent probabilities;
- For the long tails, formal values will be provided: 10% for those in the predicted
- direction, 5% for the opposite direction;
- A double probability means a double chance of occurrence;
- Probabilities are subject to Bayesian recalculation if an intermediate target is reached: if the trend is in a certain direction, the probabilities are recalculated upwards in that direction.

Under these circumstances, statistical verification can be done, post factum, on the same principles as for weather forecasts: 40% chance means that 40% of the time the forecast was correct.

Joint probabilities can be used to predict the link between securities or markets. The probabilities of each element are called marginal probabilities: for example, the proposed probabilities for the S&P and forex (e.g. EUR/USD rates). The real art is the calculation of joint probabilities: the probability that developments occur simultaneously. Two examples will show the extremes: the stock and futures price of the same security will vary almost similarly; if one takes a short position on futures, on the same security that is held in the portfolio, arbitrage/hedging results: the two positions will vary similarly but in the opposite direction.

Here we should mention that we have a different position from most proponents of modern portfolio theories, who argue that diversification is the optimal investment solution to protect the portfolio. This view is similar to arbitrage: losses are reduced, but so are profits. Investing in the stock market is not about preserving wealth; the stock market is an opportunity for the rich to get richer. Investment policy must therefore be to find the most profitable sectors–industries–firms and the optimal entry–exit moments. Diversification can occur when firms in these areas are actually chosen to mitigate specific, individual risks. But selecting zero correlated (completely uncorrelated) firms in the portfolio is an idea we have no rational reason to encourage.

7.2 Stock Forecasts Available on the Market

Although some regulators do not like binary options (Binary), (FBI), they are a good example of forecasting, even if in the short term, the evolution of the stock market. Binary options are most commonly used to predict the price of stock market securities until the end of the day (or at a later point in time, but usually very close in time). Many websites (Binaryoptions) offer the public the possibility of using these options.

Suppose we have found a way to determine the probability of the stock price trend in the coming weeks.

It should be pointed out that this distribution should not be based on the Gaussian model (which does not apply to the stock market and, for that matter, not to sports betting—where the Poisson distribution is preferred) (Dimitris Karlis, 2003), not only statistical data (which do not take trends into account, because they do not have the ability to show the evolution of the data), option pricing methods (which are based on assumptions that are not related to practice) are not useful, financial data (once they appear), general market sentiment, any unexpected events that occur should probably be taken into account. Share prices should follow probability theory to avoid the Dutch book (Jeffrey, 2004).

Therefore, this issue is completely open, the actual introduction of such bets contributes to the development of prediction procedures, both practical and theoretical.

Although there must be control (because market manipulation can occur to influence the price bet), (Anderson, 2012), the avoidance of supervision by market institutions can leave room for imagination, contributing to the free setting of quotes (they do not have to be justified, as is the case with broker/consultant forecasts).

7.3 Why There Are No Bookmakers?

Analyzing the literature, we could see that even the strategy of remaining on the winning side of the market does not give optimal returns in any conditions. As a matter of principle, the position must belong during bull periods, respectively short in bear markets. The problem arises in indecisive trading periods.

The strategies X and 0 (Turcaş, 2008) are based on the graphs point and figure with reverse box = 1 and consist of changing the position with the change of the symbol on the graph. The gain/loss is determined by counting the symbols in the same column, minus 2 (losses due to the delay of the reversal of the investment position due to the trend change), which is then multiplied by the range of variation.

Figure 7.1. shows that the strategy works well on strong trends, but is losing during trading periods. In conclusion, stock market investments do not produce sufficient returns without realistic forecasts. It follows that the development of the most accurate and realistic methods of forecasting the evolution of the market and the quotations of securities is decisive for consistent stock market results (Fig. 7.2).

Being a bet initiated by the bookmaker and bitcoin not being officially recognized as a currency, this is the best example of forecasting the evolution of the financial markets, the bet odds being determined solely on the basis of specialists' forecasts (Fig. 7.3).

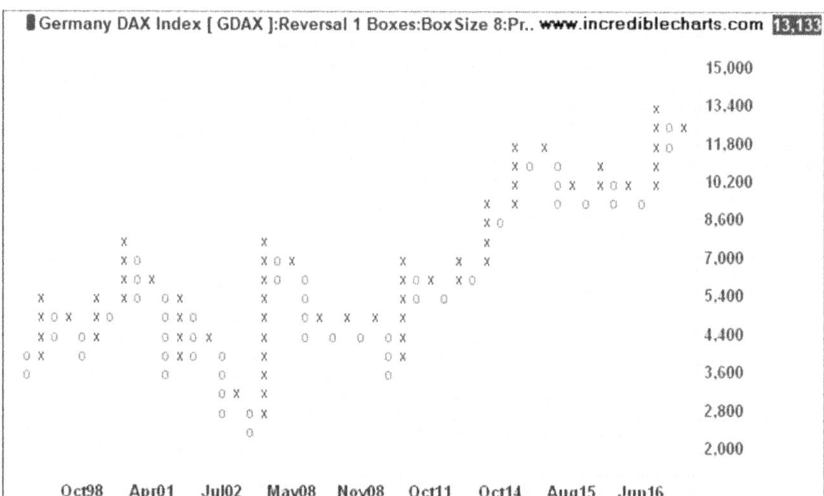

Fig. 7.1 X and 0 strategy (*Source* Own processing with the software available on the incrediblecharts.com website)

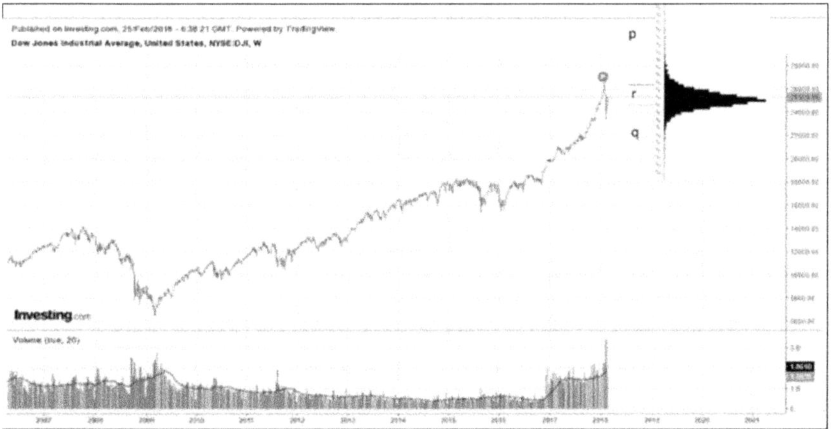

Fig. 7.2 Stock betting (*Source* Own processing)

Cryptocurrencies Specials - Bitcoin Close Price - 2018 Multiple

Bitcoin Close ... | Ethereum Clo... | Ripple Close ... | Bitcoin Close ... | Bitcoin Close ... | Mai multe

Cash Out | Reguli Combinate: RON 741,558 Reîncarcă

11 selecții			Pro toate	Contra t...		
Under $5000.01	2.38 53	2.4 305	2.46 53	2.52 58	2.56 58	2.76 314
$5000.01 - $10000	4 467	4.2 190	4.3 606	4.7 82	5.8 59	7.2 151
$10000.01 - $15000	5 290	5.5 478	6.2 96	9 178	12 582	19.5 53
$15000.01 - $20000	7 398	8 478	10 113	22 56	1000 67	
$20000.01 - $25000	18 334	19 121	21 144	690 54	1000 62	
$25000.01 - $30000	20 271	26 266	36 82	60 98	1000 105	
$30000.01 - $35000	24 265	32 204	42 83	60 93	90 61	1000 67
$35000.01 - $40000	10 58	34 221	44 73	100 65	1000 88	
$40000.01 - $45000	36 55	46 143	55 53	150 63	1000 101	
$45000.01 - $50000	38 57	48 138	55 53	250 59	1000 90	
Over $50000	13 200	19 139	20 55	27 62	1000 83	

Fig. 7.3 Betting on bitcoin (Betfair) (*Source* Own processing)

7.4 How Forecasts Can Be Used in Conjunction with Technical Analysis

Martingale strategies are known probabilistic tactics by which one ensures a certain gain, but requires potentially unlimited investments. There are many variants of martingale, for example, the one on display (Tijms, 2019). They are based on the mathematical relationship:

$$\sum_{i=0}^{n} 2^{i} = 2^{n+1} - 1 < 2^{n+1} \tag{7.1}$$

Thus, doubling the amount wagered in a game with two possible results (throwing the coin, red/black at roulette, etc.), in the end, the winner will be ensured by the fact that the amount won (double the amount wagered) ultimately exceeds the investment.

The condition of success is that the investor has an unlimited amount if the sequence of results to the contrary is long. The theory holds that martingale does not bring resounding successes to the capital market, the investor's bankruptcy being imminent under unfavorable conditions. In our approach, the theory was adapted to the scholarship. Because there is a need for a lot of data in the statistical analysis, we considered the closing prices of the DJIA in the period 27.05.1896 ÷ 09.07.2018 (31.664 input data).

We started from the hypothesis that the market has some inertia, so it is likely that if today it has risen (low), tomorrow it will keep the same variation. Of the total 31,662 daily variations analyzed, 16,023 had the same meaning as the previous day, or 50.61%. The result can be statistically relevant and can be exploited by martingale. Daily variations = increase/decrease from the previous day, which can be speculated by binary options. Although these are considered bets (and are even prohibited in some countries), the legal aspect is not relevant here: long/short positions can be adopted on the stock exchange, futures, etc.

Specialized websites generally grant a win probability of 85%, so simply betting in the blind brokerage house comes out to win statistically, in the long run. Therefore, the multiplier must be slightly larger than 2 (from the previous formula). In Table 7.1, we have presented the potential results, calculating up to 10 variations to the contrary (10 reinvestments due to successive unfavorable variations—in our case, variations to the contrary the next day).

Table 7.1 Win board martingale binary options

Simulations	*Sum*	*Gain*	*Invests*	*ROI Crude*	*ROI %*
0	2.0	4.08	2.00	2.08	104%
1	4.8	9.79	6.80	2.99	44%
2	11.5	23.50	18.32	5.18	28%
3	27.6	56.40	45.97	10.43	23%
4	66.4	135.36	112.32	23.04	21%
5	159.3	324.88	271.58	53.30	20%
6	382.2	779.70	653.78	125.92	19%
7	917.3	1,871.28	1,571.08	300.20	19%
8	2,201.5	4,491.07	3,772.58	718.49	19%
9	5,283.6	10,778.57	9,056.20	1,722.38	19%
10	12,680.7	25,868.58	21,736.87	4,131.71	19%

Source Own processing in Excel

Theoretically and in the long run, given that the probability of preserving the sense of variation is higher than that of reverse, the strategy should be winning. The problem is how many successive negative situations we can bear, given the available investment amount. The statistics of the greater number of successive days on which the variation has changed each time are as follows (Table 7.2):

There have not been 13 successive days in history in which the variation is each time of the opposite sign. In only 12 cases, there were over 10 days of successive changes (in our analysis, these days we could

Table 7.2 Likelihood of unfavorable cases

No. of days	*No. of cases*	*Probability*
6	198	0.625%
7	107	0.338%
8	46	0.145%
9	26	0.082%
10	16	0.051%
11	10	0.032%
12	2	0.006%
13	–	0.000%

Source Own processing in Excel

no longer bid because the amount to be invested exceeds our financial possibilities).

Theoretically, the analysis proves that having 12,680.70 lei, we would have lost the entire available and we would have been ruined. One observation, however: no one forces us to play to the point of bankruptcy. In just 16 cases, we would have lost the amount of 10 successive opposing days. If we stopped at level 10 and resumed from here, we had a gain of 189,463.56 lei so far. It seems a little in a century, but starting from an initial investment of 2 lei, the strategy results in winning, even if it requires a lot of patience (Table 7.3).

Obviously, one can also make the observation that there is no point in applying the strategy when the trend is strong because it is very likely that today's trend will be maintained tomorrow.

In our investor materials, we have proposed a score-based method to help investors decide. The method is shown in Fig. 7.4., and the logic is as follows:

- A few representative indicators have been selected. **P/E**, **P/BV**, **DY**, and **PEG** link the technical analysis (stock price) to the fundamental

Table 7.3 Earnings table

No days to the contrary	*No. of cases*	*Probability (%)*	*Unit gain*	*Total win*
0	16,023	50.606	2.08	33,327.84
1	8,020	25.330	2.99	23,995.84
2	4,015	12.681	5.18	20,800.91
3	1,899	5.998	10.43	19,814.01
4	877	2.770	23.04	20,207.31
5	422	1.333	53.30	22,492.34
6	198	0.625	125.92	24,931.86
7	107	0.338	300.20	32,121.87
8	46	0.145	718.49	33,050.57
9	26	0.082	1,722.38	44,781.81
10	16	0.051	4,131.71	66,107.30
11	10	0.032	−12,680.68	−126,806.76
12	2	0.006	−12,680.68	−25,361.35
13	–	0.000	−12,680.68	0.00
Total	**31.661**	**100,00**		**189.463,56**

Source Own processing in Excel

		Valoare				Sell										Hold										Buy	
Indic.	Rec.	Emitent	Calcul	Punctaj	Min	-1,0	-0,9	-0,8	-0,7	-0,6	-0,5	-0,4	-0,3	-0,2	-0,1	0,0	0,1	0,2	0,3	0,4	0,5	0,6	0,7	0,8	0,9	1,0	Max
PER	↘	3,00	1,0	25%	5																					1,0	30
P/BV	↘	1,00	0,6	25%	0,5																	0,6					3
DY	↗	5,0%	-0,5	10%	0%						-0,5																20%
PEG	↘	2.650,7%	-1,0	5%	0	-1,0																					1
Renta	↘	-1,5%	1,0	35%	0%																					1,0	20%
Σ			0,7	100%	Final																		0,7				

Fig. 7.4 Combining indicators for the investment decision. (*Source* Own processing in Excel)

analysis (financial results, their evolution, equity value). **Return** represents the total stock market return (final price minus initial price plus any dividends or other benefits from holding the shares in the last year) and is a purely technical indicator.

- The recommendation (**Rec.**) has been interpreted according to the value of the indicator. If a high value of the indicator draws attention to the overvaluation of the share, the recommendation is to sell, i.e. ↘. If a lower value signals overvaluation, the recommendation is to buy when the indicator rises, i.e.↗.
- A normal range has been established, between Max and Min. Indicator values outside these limits will be considered as having the extreme values mentioned.
- **The score** represents the weight of each criterion in the total ($\sum = 100\%$). Practical values should be taken from interviewing market participants and from investor experience. For the present study, we interviewed only a few brokers, as the method requires a wider panel of opinions.
- The numerical values of the indicators in the **Min** ÷ **Max** range were rescaled in proportion to the size of the range. The calculation formulas are:

  Calculation=ROUND(IF(I4<L4;1;IF(I4>AH4;-1;1-2*(I4-L4)/(AH4-L4)));1 for indicators ↘ and

  Calculation=ROUND(IF(I6<L6;-1;IF(I6>AH6;1;2*(I6-L6)/(AH6-L6)-1));1) for indicators ↗

  where column I is the value of the issuer indicator, L is the column with **Min** values and AH with **Max** values.
- Thus, each indicator generated a recommendation between **Sell–Hold–Buy**, with investors facing the issuer's position relative to

the market (the extreme values of the indicators are taken from the specific market) in each chapter.

- The Excel program allows automatic coloring of cells according to their value, so the recommendation is even more visible: from **Sell**, then **Hold**, to **Buy.**
- The final recommendation results from the weighted sum of the initial recommendations, either based on the **score** proposed by the consultant or the one chosen by the investor.

The proposed method works well if the scoring is set as close as possible to the views of market participants).

7.5 Finis Coronat Opus

Trying to beat the market is tantamount to wanting to score more goals on your own than your team. To beat in the long run, the buy and hold strategy is something normal, and any technical analyst can succeed. To compare yourself to the market means to use stock indices as a benchmark (target),

portfolio selection remains an open issue. But as long as the evaluation does not tell us anything about the predicted evolution of quotations when academic theories do not yield better results than the common 1/n, and the technical and fundamental analysis is not found in a coherent logic of investment recommendations.

We have proposed to approach forecasts (and implicitly market analysis) from the perspective of betting theory. In our approach, we remain of the opinion that the one who will be able to predict, with statistically good results, the exchange rates of securities and future quotations is the one who has understood the capital market well.

Regarding the betting strategies, we propose the realization of a coherent system that would determine what odds are useful for various quotes of a title in a week or a month (no less than it's gambling, no more I am not a fortune teller), as well as a system of modifying them along the way (different or not from the Bayesian model) we think it would represent the full understanding of the laws of the stock markets.

References

Anderson, R. M., Eom, K. S., Hahn, A. B., & Park, J. -H. (2012). *Sources of stock return autocorrelation*. UC Berkeley.

Brooks, A. (2012). *Trading price action trends. Technical analysis of price charts bar by bar for the serious trader.* John Wiley & Sons, Inc.

Dimitris Karlis, I. N. (2003). *Analysis of sports data by using bivariate Poisson models.* The Statistician.

Dumiter, F., & Turcaş, F. (2022). Theoretical and empirical underpinnings regarding stock market forecasts and predictions. *Studia Universitatis Vasile Goldiş Arad-Economics Series, 32*(1), 1–19.

Elton, E. J., Gruber, M. J., Brown, S. J., & Goetzman, W. N. (2014). *Modern portfolio theory and investment analysis*— (9th ed.). John Wiley & Sons Inc.

Fabozzi, F. J., & Markowitz, H. M. (2011). *The theory and practice of investment management. Asset allocation, valuation, portfolio construction, and strategies—second edition*. John Wiley & Sons, Inc.

Fabozzi, F. J., Focardi, S. M., Rachev, S. T., Arshanapalli, B. G., & Hochstotter, M. (2014). *The basics of financial econometrics. Tools, concepts and asset management applications.* John Wiley & Sons, Inc.

Jeffrey, R. (2004). *Subjective probability.* Cambridge University Press.

Jimon, ŞA., Dumiter, F. C., & Balteş, N. (2021). *Financial sustainability of pension systems*. Springer.

Pachamanova, D. A., & Fabozzi, F. J. (2010). *Simulation and optimization in finance. Modeling with Matlab, @Risk, or VBA.* John Wiley & Sons, Inc.

Stewart, S. D., Piros, C. D., & Heisler, J. C. (2019). *Portfolio management: Theory and practice*— (2nd ed.). John Wiley & Sons Inc.

Tijms, H. (2019). *Surprises in probability seventeen short stories.* CRC Press Taylor & Francis Group.

Turcaş, F. (2008). Strategia X şi 0. *Revista AATROM*.

Turcaş, F., Dumiter, F., Brezeanu, P., Fărcaş, P., & Coroiu, S. (2017). Practical aspects of portfolio selection and optimization on the capital market. *Economic Research-Ekonomska Istrazivanja, 30*(1), 14–30.

Zheng, X., & Chen, B. M. (2013). *Stock market modeling and forecasting.* Springer.

CHAPTER 8

Stages of Technical Analysis

Abstract These are the steps leading to the conclusion on the timing of investment, volume, holding period, and warning signals. A summary of the main elements of technical analysis, presented in the natural order of their use, will conclude the paper. We will remind you that technical analysis, although a powerful tool, is not an Aladdin's lamp: it can give guidance, but it cannot predict exactly the future. The vast majority of investors look at the same charts but do not understand the same thing. Some sell, some buy, each looking for the best result. We just have to position ourselves on the right side of the market: follow the trend. But we must also follow some basic rules: let your profits run and cut your losses short. After all, with a little discipline and basic knowledge, success should not be long in coming: going from 50–50% success to 70–30%, while difficult, should encourage anyone to go to 75%, 80%.

Keywords Investment strategies · Warning signals · Holding period · Volume · Time investment

Cui et al. (2012) developed an empirical study that tackles the paths and movements of several investment strategies in sequential order. The authors' study focuses especially on the high-frequency environment which confers some answers regarding several techniques and strategies.

F. C. Dumiter and F. M. Turcaş, *Technical Analysis Applications*,
https://doi.org/10.1007/978-3-031-27416-9_8

A literature review study created by Scott et al. (2016) tackles the modern perspectives of technical analyses. The authors deal in their study with the complex problem of behavioral economics, the action of the players in the market, and market behavior.

A very insightful empirical study represents the work of Bartnik et al. (2017) in which the authors deal with the application of CHP and heating as related to sequential investment strategies. The authors have developed several mathematical models in order to evaluate and assess the soundness of the sequential investment strategies in the energy market.

Zaremba and Shemer (2018) applied several research techniques and tactics established to reinvent the nature and structure of technical analysis. The authors have implemented price-based strategies for creating an empirical guide toward the research techniques which encompass asset pricing.

An interesting practitioner's guide toward developing several trading strategies applied to China was developed by Zhang (2018). The author tackles very interesting topics with regard to an optimal investment portfolio: building blocks, applied pricing curves, regulatory regimes portfolio objectives, and risk management.

Oliver (2019) study the stock trends applied to different markets. Based on practical experience proved in the stock market the author deals with some interesting aspects such as strategies, chart patterns, candlesticks, and several indicators.

In the aftermath, Schlotmann and Czubatinski (2019) developed an easy-to-read and use guide on technical analysis for practitioners and beginners. In their study, the authors focus on psychological factors, mass psychology related to the traders' beliefs and movements on the stock market.

Bulkowski (2021) has developed the most comprehensive stock market guide toward chart trends and patterns. Based on the vast empirical and practical experience the author has developed an interesting study that is easy to understand in terms of pattern trends, evolution, and statistical performances.

One of the most interesting and insightful studies regarding stock trends is developed by Edwards et al. (2021). The authors analyze and assess the whole range of investment strategies applied to technical analysis with a special focus on commodity charts, formations, patterns, and channels.

Saramento and Horta (2021) developed an interesting insight regarding computational intelligence in sequential investment strategies. The authors developed an automated learning machine strategy that proposes pairs trading, pairs selection, and the implementation of a proposed trading model.

8.1 The Market in General, Macroeconomic Considerations

Technical analysis uses charts of past stock performance to predict future performance, based on the consideration that stock market behavior has characteristics that are preserved over time.

Statistical analysis is also based on past movements, assuming that the market is informationally efficient in the sense defined by Famma; i.e. the securities price fully (or at least largely) reflects all the information on the valuation of the securities.

The fundamental analysis only considers the economic reality in the company, on the reasoning that the stock market trend only reflects the public's opinion on the prospects of the share, and is thus suitable for non-controlling shares but not for the value of the company for the majority holders.

Valuation approaches use either equity value (e.g. by summing assets), return value (by income, e.g. DFC method), or market value (usually by indicators and multipliers applied to comparables).

What all these theories omit is consideration of macroeconomic developments. In other words, they focus on the company itself, but stock market developments are also decisively influenced by the economic environment. Why? Because in the stock market the availability and cost of money matter immensely.

There is an empirical theory that the stock market precedes the economic cycle by ½ ÷ 1 year. Looking at Fig. 8.1, we tend to accept this statement.

8.2 Monthly–Weekly–Daily Charts

All technical analysis must follow top-down analysis: from the general to the particular. This is the natural order: first, we look at the general trend, then we look at momentary movements. Long-term investors only look

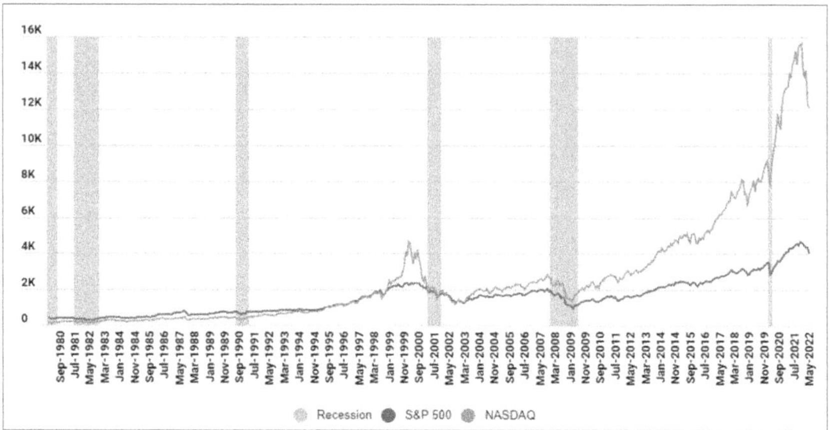

Fig. 8.1 Stock performance during recessions (*Source* www.fool.com/research/stock-performance-recessions/)

at monthly or weekly charts; speculators only look at daily or even shorter time frames.

Indeed, money can be made from short moves, sometimes even contrary to the general trend, but we must never forget which cycle we are in. In Fig. 8.2, we can see that there have been bounces even during the worst financial crisis of 2008 ÷ 2009. However, speculation and portfolio management must be handled completely differently than in growth cycles (Fig. 8.3). Attention, investment horizon, the amount invested, and influence of news are all differences between the two cases, which need to be handled completely differently.

Conflicting stock market recommendations are encountered on different timeframes. Here is an example, taken from investing.com (Fig. 8.4). Based on the mathematical results of applying technical analysis indicators, the site automatically generated the recommendations mentioned for Banca Transilvania—the largest bank in Romania.

8.3 Trends–Support/Resistance–Channels. Volume

Why do the conclusions vary in different time frames (from daily to monthly)? Because the data considered in the calculations also differ radically. Is this a problem? Possibly not: if for example the issuer is on a

Fig. 8.2 Upside during the subprime crisis (*Source* investing.com)

Fig. 8.3 Bull market (*Source* investing.com)

major uptrend, but has a minor downturn. Let's check this with "pen to paper" (Fig. 8.5).

We will therefore turn to the charts generated on the website of the Bucharest Stock Exchange, bvb.ro, on the symbol TLV (Fig. 8.6).

Long-term TLV is clearly on a multi-year uptrend (major trend)—top chart. Being near the trend line, there are two investment options: either

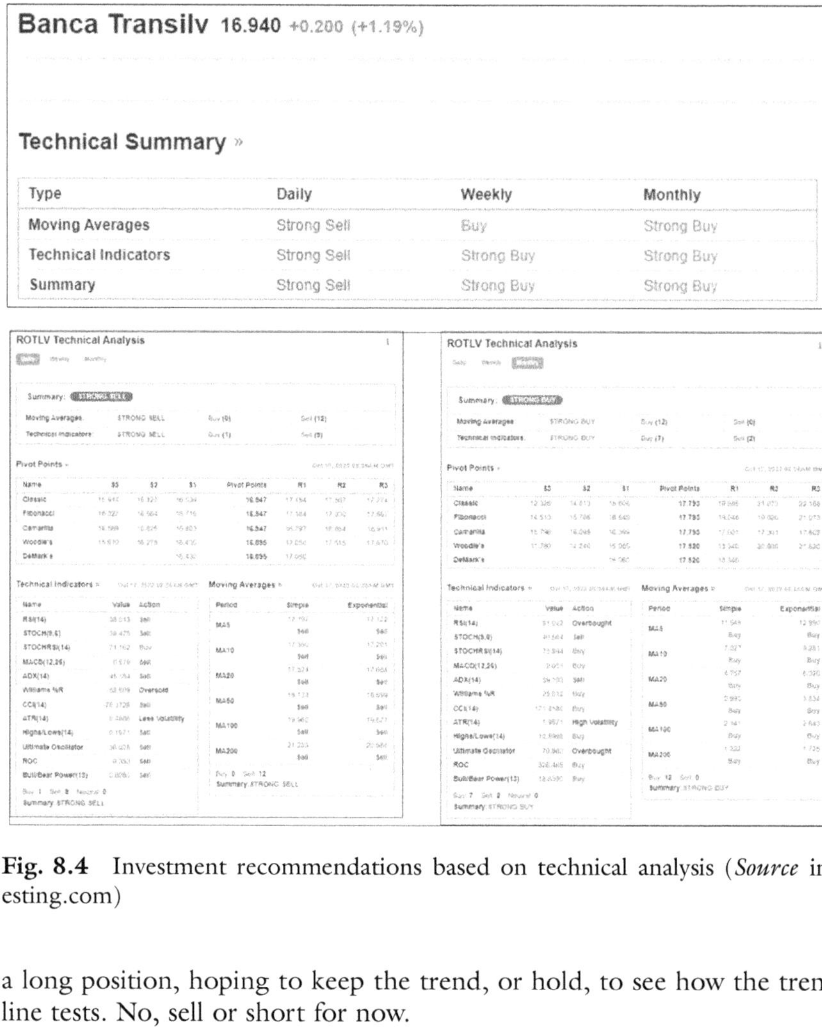
Banca Transilv 16.940 +0.200 (+1.19%)

Technical Summary »

Type	Daily	Weekly	Monthly
Moving Averages	Strong Sell	Buy	Strong Buy
Technical Indicators	Strong Sell	Strong Buy	Strong Buy
Summary	Strong Sell	Strong Buy	Strong Buy

Fig. 8.4 Investment recommendations based on technical analysis (*Source* investing.com)

a long position, hoping to keep the trend, or hold, to see how the trend line tests. No, sell or short for now.

In the short-term—bottom chart, daily—TLV is still obviously on a secondary downtrend that is not even close to being broken. So the recommendation can only be hold.

The bottom line, at least in our opinion, is to get your money ready and wait for the likely resumption of the stock market rally.

Even more eloquent than the trend lines are the channels: the quotation curve is framed by two parallel lines: one is the trend line, and the

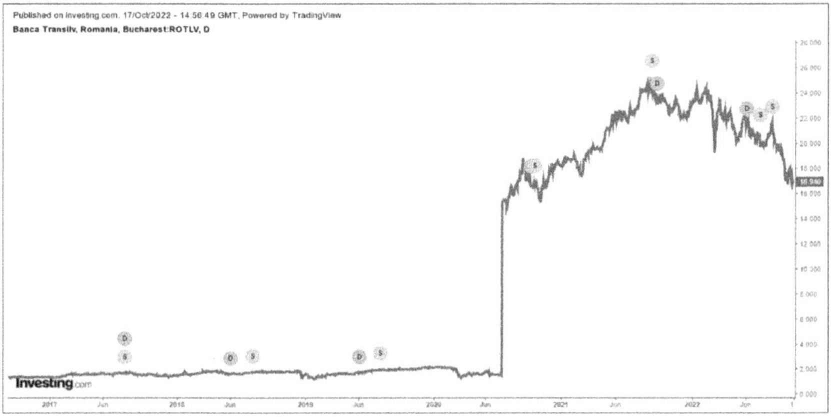

Fig. 8.5 Unadjusted chart on TLV (*Source* investing.com)

other follows it at some distance. The conclusion here is even better: as long as the chart stays inside the channel, the price will bounce from the lower to the upper channel and vice versa, making the evolution easy to predict.

The chart in Fig. 8.7 shows that the DJIA falls in price channels, which makes its evolution predictable over medium time intervals.

The support and resistance thresholds are useful to predict how far movements are expected to go, depending on past extremes (Fig. 8.8).

Volume is also important because it confirms or denies momentum (the strength of the trend). Figure 8.9 indicates that the divergence between price and volume signals a weakening of the trend, which makes a reversal to be expected.

The conclusion is that trend lines, thresholds, and price channels foreshadow the main price movements quite well and are useful to decide the overall market condition.

8.4 Patterns

Patterns do not appear as often as trend lines, but when they do emerge they are immediately recognized by those concerned (brokers, investors, analysts) and therefore have an important psychological power.

Fig. 8.6 TLV monthly and daily charts (*Source* investing.com)

Fig. 8.7 Price channels on the DJIA chart (*Source* investing.com)

Fig. 8.8 Resistance and supports are price targets (*Source* investing.com)

On an obvious uptrend, the DJIA forms an ascending triangle—a moment of accumulation before the upswing resumes (Fig. 8.10).

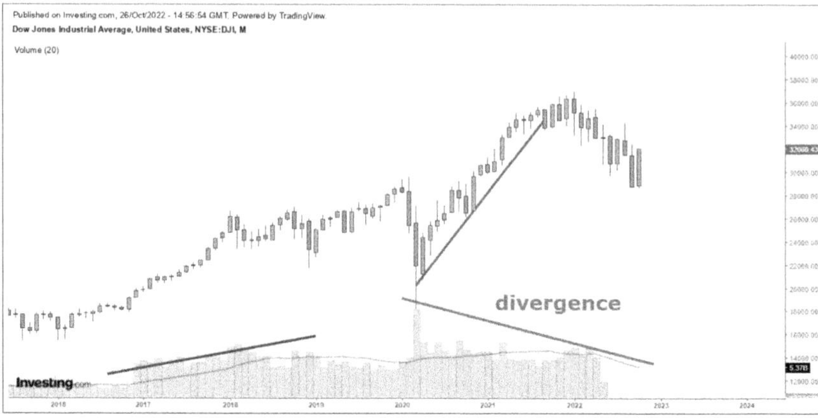

Fig. 8.9 Importance of Volume (*Source* investing.com)

Fig. 8.10 Triangle (*Source* investing.com)

8.5 Moving Averages–Indicators–Oscillators–Opposing Views

An important warning signal of trend termination is the intersection of moving averages (Fig. 8.11).

Fig. 8.11 Moving average intersection (*Source* investing.com)

Although they are clear benchmarks, the average intersections have a shortcoming: if the intersection lines are too close together, they become too numerous; if they are too far apart, the intersections lag far behind the actual change in trend. However, their mere proximity may signal a moment of attention.

A better analysis, also based on moving averages, is done by the MACD, where the intersection of the lines (averages) shows very good signals of trend reversals (Fig. 8.12).

Of the more than 100 indicators and oscillators available on trading and analysis platforms, we have discussed here the RSI, which indicates over- and under-sold moments, respectively (Fig. 8.13).

Our advice on these indicators and oscillators is to select those that you understand and that are confirmed for the selected securities.

8.6 Comparisons–Correlation–Probabilities

For modern portfolio theory enthusiasts, we consider technical analysis to be the best way to predict the important elements: expected return—through the graphically determined price target; variance—through Bollinger bands; correlation—through the comparison of the evolution of securities.

Fig. 8.12 MACD (*Source* Chart: investing.com)

Fig. 8.13 RSI (*Source* investing.com)

Let's take an example: 2 securities on the US market—AAPL and MSFT.

From the first chart in Fig. 8.14, it is clear that the expected return is higher for Microsoft compared to Apple. The second graph (logarithmic) shows that the titles are highly correlated over the last period. Finally, by plotting the Bollinger bands, we can see the variance, which has increased for both companies in the last period.

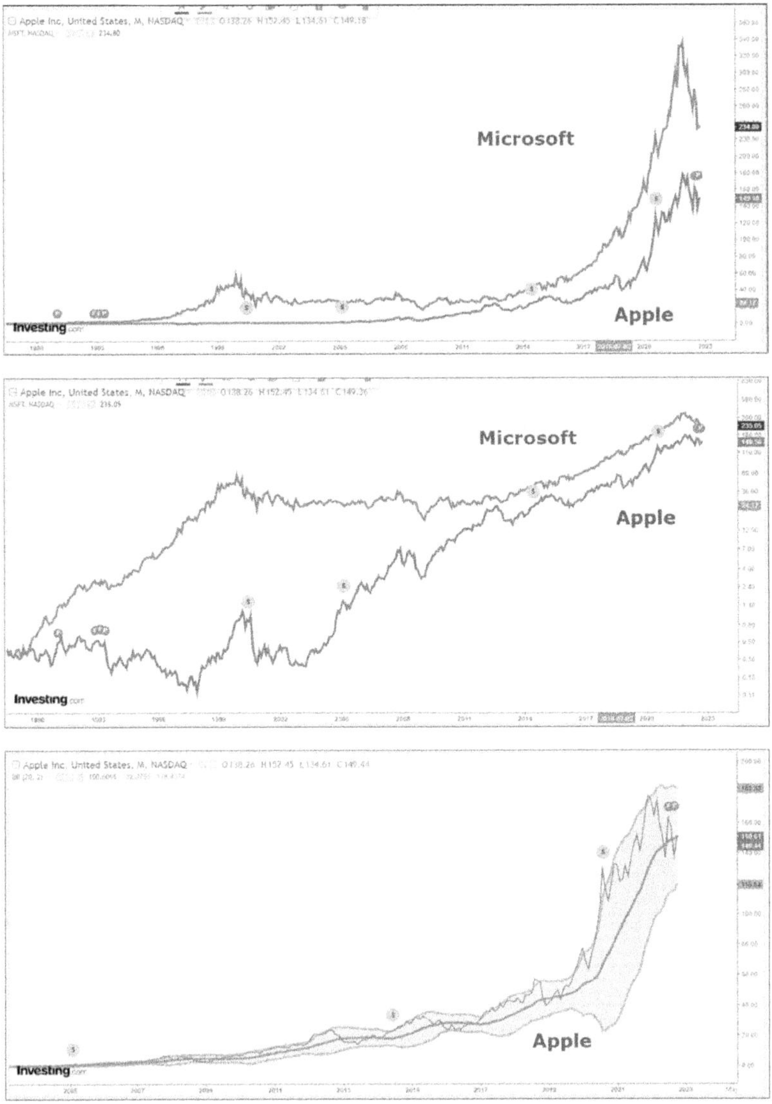

Fig. 8.14 Graphical determination of the main parameters for MPT (*Source* inv esting.com)

8.7 Finis Coronat Opus

Although not a universal panacea, technical analysis gives us valuable clues as to the existence and strength of trends, their possible change, and price targets.

Each stock and period (trending, trading) has suitable indicators, oscillators, and appropriate related variables. Only by tracking them, experience and trials can optimal solutions be configured.

The technical analysis starts from the general economic environment, which determines the volume and availability of money that can be floated on the stock exchange and the evolution of the field and industry to which the issuer belongs.

The long-term analysis determines the multi-year trend and the long-term trend. Forward-looking investors only follow this segment because they are not interested in short-term speculation. However, even for them, it's not all the same when they buy the asset—an immediate drop after purchase is not encouraging for investors or traders. Therefore, weekly analysis can give medium-term signals, because any major trend, even the strongest ones, has moments of reversal or excessive momentum.

In the short run, speculators follow daily or even shorter charts; personally, however, we appreciate that the advantages of technical analysis (general statistical conclusions on the stock's evolution, investors' reaction to chart signals, feedback on news and releases, etc.) are lost on such short intervals. However, some assets can only be analyzed on a graphical or statistical basis, because either fundamental analysis does not reach such high accuracies (e.g. forex), or it does not even have a purpose (e.g. crypto).

References

Bartnik, R., Buryn, Z., & Hnydiuk-Stefan, A. (2017). *Investment strategies in heating and CHP: Mathematical models*. Springer Cham.

Bulkowski, T. (2021). *Encyclopedia of chart patterns* (3rd ed.). Wiley.

Cui, H., Zhang, Y., & Chen, H. (2012). Learning sequential investment strategy in high-frequency environment. In *ISICA 2012: Computational Intelligence and Intelligent Systems* (pp. 432–439).

Edwards, R., Magee, J., & Bassetti, W. H. C. (2021). *Technical analysis of stock trends* (11th ed.). CRC Press.

Oliver, P. (2019). *Technical analysis of stock trends (investment series)*. Independently published.

Sarmento, S. M., & Horta, N. (2021). *A machine learning-based pairs trading investment strategy*. Springer Cham.
Schlotmann, R., & Czubatinski, M. (2019). *Trading: Technical analysis master-class: Master the financial markets*. Independently published.
Scott, G., Carr, M., & Cremonie, M. (2016). *Technical analysis: Modern perspectives*. CFA Institute Research Foundation.
Zaremba, A., & Shemer, J. K. (2018). *Price-based investment strategies: How research discoveries reinvented technical analysis*. Palgrave Macmillan Cham.
Zhang, X. (2018). *Capital markets trading and investment strategies in China: A practitioner's guide*. Springer Singapore.

Index

F. C. Dumiter and F. M. Turcaş, *Technical Analysis Applications*,
https://doi.org/10.1007/978-3-031-27416-9

GPSR Compliance
The European Union's (EU) General Product Safety Regulation (GPSR) is a set of rules that requires consumer products to be safe and our obligations to ensure this.

If you have any concerns about our products, you can contact us on

ProductSafety@springernature.com

In case Publisher is established outside the EU, the EU authorized representative is:

Springer Nature Customer Service Center GmbH
Europaplatz 3
69115 Heidelberg, Germany

www.ingramcontent.com/pod-product-compliance
Ingram Content Group UK Ltd.
Pitfield, Milton Keynes, MK11 3LW, UK
UKHW020836290926
15470UKWH00004B/1380
* 9 7 8 3 0 3 1 2 7 4 1 5 2 *